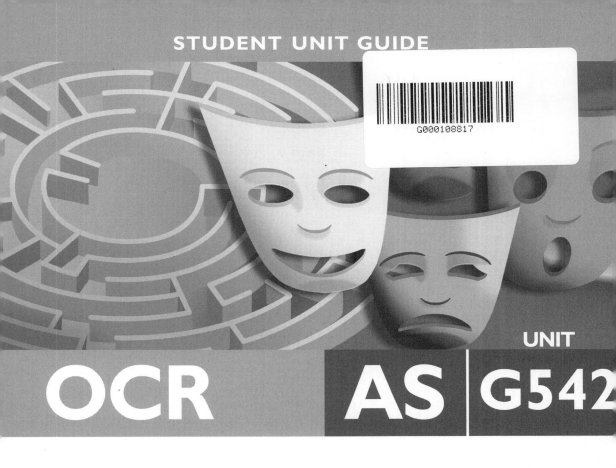

OCR

AS | G542

UNIT

Psychology

Core Studies

David Clarke

Philip Allan Updates, an imprint of Hodder Education, an Hachette UK Company, Market Place, Deddington, Oxfordshire OX15 0SE

Orders

Bookpoint Ltd, 130 Milton Park, Abingdon, Oxfordshire OX14 4SB
tel: 01235 827720
fax: 01235 400454
e-mail: uk.orders@bookpoint.co.uk

Lines are open 9.00 a.m.–5.00 p.m., Monday to Saturday, with a 24-hour message answering service. You can also order through the Philip Allan Updates website: www.philipallan.co.uk

ISBN 978-0-340-95959-6

First printed 2008
Impression number 5 4 3
Year 2012 2011 2010 2009

This guide has been written specifically to support students preparing for the OCR AS Psychology Unit G542 examination. The content has been neither approved nor endorsed by OCR and remains the sole responsibility of the author.

Typeset by Phoenix Photosetting, Chatham, Kent
Printed by MPG Books, Bodmin

Hachette UK's policy is to use papers that are natural, renewable and recyclable products and made from wood grown in sustainable forests. The logging and manufacturing processes are expected to conform to the environmental regulations of the country of origin.

Contents

Introduction

■ ■ ■

Content Guidance

■ ■ ■

Questions and Answers

Introduction

About this guide

This book is a guide to Unit G542 (Core Studies) of the new OCR AS specification. Unit G542 combines Core Studies 1 (Module 2540) and Core Studies 2 (Module 2541) from the old specification.

This unit guide is not a textbook, but it is an aid to help you through the course and your revision. The emphasis is on informing you about exactly what you need to do and what you need to know to be successful in the examinations.

This guide has three sections:
- **Introduction.** This contains revision tips and suggests how you can organise your studies. It includes a look at what you need from each core study.
- **Content guidance.** The core studies illustrate the central approaches of psychology: cognitive psychology, developmental psychology, social psychology, physiological psychology, and the psychology of individual differences. It also gives details of the issues and perspectives that run through the course. Many marks can be gained from some simple comments of evaluation. This section helps you to develop your own evaluative skills, and therefore to get a better grade.
- **Questions and answers.** The answers provided here are not intended to be model answers, so don't learn them and try to reproduce them in your own examination. The best thing to do is to look at the responses and the comments of the examiner, and then try to apply the best techniques to your own answers. You might find it useful to attempt your own answer to the specimen questions before you read the examiner's comments.

Examination guidance

The Core Studies examination is a 2-hour paper divided into three sections.

Section A consists of 15 short-answer questions, each worth 4 marks. Commonly, questions are divided into two parts, each worth 2 marks. Section A is worth 60 of the total 120 marks. Approximately 45 minutes should be spent answering questions from this section. This equates to 3 minutes for reading, thinking about and writing the answer to each question. Think about how much you can write in 3 minutes. There is no point writing 20 lines for the first question and then running out of time at the end of the section.

Some Section A questions require very short answers: two points for 2 marks; others, such as those that start with 'Describe' or 'Explain', require more detail and can be worth 4 marks. Think about how much will you need to write to guarantee all 4 marks. In these cases, one sentence is not enough.

Section A is the same as the previous Module 2540 paper, so past questions and mark schemes can be used to prepare for the new Section A.

Section B consists of one compulsory question about a specific core study. The question has several parts, typically worth 2, 6 or 8 marks, making a combined total of 36 marks for the question. Approximately 45 minutes should be spent on this question.

This section is entirely new and there are no previous papers like it. Its aim is to allow candidates to write more about what is good and not so good about a specific core study.

Section C consists of two questions, each relating to an approach, perspective or issue. It has four parts, worth 2, 4, 6 and 12 marks, making a total of 24 marks overall. Approximately 30 minutes should be spent on this section.

This section is similar to the previous Module 2541 paper, but with some improvements. However, past questions can be used to get an idea of question types, but note that the new mark scheme is different.

Candidates often finish writing ahead of time. However, there is no prize for finishing first, and candidates who finish early will probably not do as well as they expect. Which type of candidate are you? Are you the one who finishes early, or do you give that little bit more detail, guaranteeing that you will achieve the maximum mark for each question?

On the other hand, whatever you do, don't run out of time. Be strict with yourself. Try testing yourself so you know exactly how much you can write in the time allowed. Ask your teacher to give you test essays on exam questions.

The table below summarises the mark allocation, time allocation and recommended length of answer for the Core Studies examination.

Section	Mark allocation	Time spent on the question	Amount of writing
Section A	60 marks	45 mins	2+ sides of A4
Section B	36 marks	45 mins	3 sides of A4
Section C	24 marks	30 mins	2+ sides of A4
Totals	**120 marks**	**120 mins**	**8 sides of A4**

Before you start

You have decided to study psychology because you have some fascination with the way that people behave and interact with others. You may have burning questions about life and the universe, or wonder why we sleep, or what would happen if your brain were split into two. Studying psychology may lead you to look at the world in a different way, and it may even lead you to think about things most people never even consider.

My passion for psychology began when I studied the subject at A-level. Within 2 weeks I knew what I wanted to do for the rest of my life. I hope you will develop the same fascination. You will find that psychology won't answer all your questions and, while in most ways it will exceed your expectations, it won't meet them in others. Contrary to popular misconceptions, during the course, you will not learn how to 'analyse' people or read their minds.

Before you start the course you will probably know nothing about psychology, but, then, neither will the other 17,000 students following the OCR specification. You will need to develop two things: subject knowledge and an ability to synthesise it (i.e. examination technique). My job is to point you in the right direction — you and your teacher can work on the knowledge part, and this guide will help you to put it all together for the examination.

What is OCR psychology?

The current OCR specification contains 15 core studies that will give you a broad introduction to psychology and also introduce you to methodologies, issues and debates. Some of the core studies are old — for example, the Freud study is from 1909, the work of Bandura et al. from 1961, and that of Rosenhan from 1973. However, others were published more recently, such as the Reicher and Haslam study (2006), reflecting the latest research available.

The core studies are grouped by a common theme into five categories called **approaches**. For example, the **developmental approach** includes three studies that look at different aspects of child development. The approaches are:

- cognitive
- developmental
- physiological
- social
- individual differences

Organising your work

You can divide your folders into sections for each of the five approaches above. You could also include an extra section for practical work or investigations and assessed work for that unit. Another section can be added for core studies assessed work — for example, all your essays. You could also create a summary sheet of the key features of each study and place it in the appropriate section in your folder.

Core studies

Below is a list of all the core studies as they appear in the specification. The studies are grouped by the appropriate approach. The author(s) and article title are given, followed by the name of the journal in which the study was originally published. Be careful to use the correct article, because sometimes there are variations. For example, the Baron-Cohen study on the OCR specification is that from 1997, and not the updated 2001 version.

Cognitive psychology

Baron-Cohen, S., Jolliffe, T., Mortimore, C. and Robertson, M. (1997) 'Another advanced test of theory of mind: evidence from very high functioning adults with autism or Asperger's syndrome', *Journal of Child Psychology and Psychiatry*, Vol. 38, pp. 813–22.

Loftus, E. and Palmer, J. (1974) 'Reconstruction of automobile destruction', *Journal of Verbal Learning and Verbal Behaviour*, Vol. 13, pp. 585–89.

Savage-Rumbaugh, S. (1986) 'Spontaneous symbol acquisition and communicative use by pygmy chimpanzees', *Journal of Experimental Psychology: General 1986*, Vol. 115, No. 3, pp. 211–35.

Developmental psychology

Bandura, A., Ross, D. and Ross, S. (1961) 'Transmission of aggression through imitation of aggressive models', *Journal of Abnormal and Social Psychology*, Vol. 63, pp. 375–82.

Freud, S. (1909) 'Analysis of a phobia of a five-year-old boy', *Pelican Freud Library*, Vol. 8, Case Histories 1.

Samuel, J. and Bryant, P. (1984) 'Asking only one question in the conservation experiment', *Journal of Child Psychology and Psychiatry*, Vol. 25, pp. 315–18.

Physiological psychology

Dement, W. and Kleitman, N. (1957) 'The relation of eye movements during sleep to dream activity', *Journal of Experimental Psychology*, Vol. 53, No. 5, pp. 339–46.

Maguire, E. A., Gadian, D. G., Johnsrude, I. S., Good, C. D., Ashburner, J., Frackowiak, R. S. and Frith, C. D. (2000) 'Navigation-related structural changes in the hippocampi of taxi drivers', *Proceedings of the National Academy of Science, USA*, Vol. 97, pp. 4398–403.

Sperry, R. (1968) 'Hemisphere deconnection and unity in consciousness', *American Psychologist*, Vol. 23, pp. 723–33.

Social psychology

Milgram, S. (1963) 'Behavioural study of obedience', *Journal of Abnormal and Social Psychology*, Vol. 67, pp. 371–78.

Piliavin, I., Rodin, J. and Piliavin, J. (1969) 'Good Samaritanism: an underground phenomenon?', *Journal of Personality and Social Psychology*, Vol. 13, No. 4, pp. 289–99.

Reicher, S. and Haslam, S. A. (2006) 'Rethinking the psychology of tyranny. The BBC prison study', *British Journal of Social Psychology*, Vol. 45, pp. 1–40.

Psychology of individual differences

Griffiths, M. D. (1994) 'The role of cognitive bias and skill in fruit machine gambling', *British Journal of Psychology*, Vol. 85, pp. 351–69.

Rosenhan, D. (1973) 'On being sane in insane places', *Science*, Vol. 197, pp. 250–58.

Thigpen, C. and Cleckley, H. (1954) 'A case of multiple personality', *Journal of Abnormal and Social Psychology*, Vol. 49, pp. 135–51.

You do not need to remember the full list of references. Where there are one or two authors, remember their names. If there are three or more authors, then you can use the first name and 'et al.': this means 'and all' and is a common abbreviation used in psychology. It is desirable to remember dates, but it is not essential and you will not get marks in the exam for doing so. You can also refer to each core study in a simplified way, rather than remembering the whole title. For example: Sperry, R. (1968) 'Hemisphere deconnection and unity in consciousness', *American Psychologist*, 23, pp. 723–33 can be abbreviated to 'Sperry (split brain)'.

This is perfectly acceptable and will save you a lot of time. You may even find that your teacher uses these abbreviations, and they could appear in the examination questions.

Core studies texts

In an examination question you can be asked about any aspect of a core study as it appears in the original publication. It is best to have a copy of the original study, as not all textbooks cover the studies in full and they can be misleading. You cannot be asked questions about something that is not mentioned in the original article. However, you should be aware that some of the original articles are heavy-going, and it is difficult to summarise their main points.

As a teacher, I recommend that you use textbooks and the internet to access alternative explanations and summaries of the studies.

What you need to know about core studies

As well as knowing about the core studies themselves, you also need to know about *approaches*, *methods*, *issues* and *perspectives*. The following table summarises everything that you need to cover.

Approaches	Methods	Issues	Perspectives
Cognitive	Laboratory experiments Field experiment	Ethics	Behaviourism
Social	Case studies	Ecological validity	Psychodynamic
Physiological	Self-reports	Longitudinal and snapshot	
Developmental	Observation	Quantitative and qualitative data	
Individual differences	Methodological issues: • Reliability • Validity		

You can be asked questions on any of the areas mentioned in the table, in addition to questions about the core studies. The following section summarises what you need to know about each study.

(1) Background to the studies (the context)

The background or context explains the reasons why a particular piece of research was conducted. The research may be a response to an earlier study. It could have been done to support a theory proposed by the author or someone else, or to investigate further or explain a real-life event.

A crucial question for both teachers and students is 'How much background is needed?' The OCR specification states: 'This need not be detailed, but sufficient to allow understanding of why the study was done.' It is not necessary to know the context of the research in great detail, but rather the gist of the background, along with an understanding of how it all fits together. Refer to the table on p. 11 to help clarify this, after considering the related points (2) and (3) below.

(2) The theory or theories on which studies are based

Studies are often based on a particular theory or theories. For example, in 1960, Stanley Schachter proposed the **two-factor theory** of emotion. In 1962, along with Jerome Singer, he conducted a piece of research designed to support the theory. Sometimes, the reverse occurs, where research is conducted and a theory is then proposed to explain the findings. The 'subway Samaritans' study by Piliavin et al. illustrates this point. In this study, the researchers found no diffusion of responsibility, which was contrary to their expectations. To explain bystander behaviour, they proposed that everyone considers the costs and benefits involved in helping or not helping a person in need.

(3) Other relevant theories and/or research

A piece of research does not occur in isolation, and sometimes many variations of the same study are carried out. Research is often conducted several years after a study to re-examine the phenomenon in question. The research on the BBC prison study by Reicher and Haslam was conducted in 2000 (but published later) to re-examine the claims made by Zimbardo on 'the psychology of tyranny', following his prison simulation experiment in 1973.

There are three ways of looking at this. First, the OCR specification states that: 'Candidates will be asked questions relating to: theories and research surrounding the core studies', but it does not specify what you need. This means that any relevant theory could be covered, but in most cases it is evident which theory is being referred to — for example, the Reicher and Haslam study is based on the Zimbardo experiment. However, it does not have to be a theory; it could be relevant research. For example, the Milgram study of obedience to authority will never be replicated in its original format because it is too unethical, but it has been done as a virtual-reality simulation (see Slater, M. et al. 2006).

Putting (1), (2) and (3) above together, you could construct a reference table on theory and research like the one below. This need not be complex (or even complete). The table below shows just three studies, but you can do it for every study.

Prior research/event/theory	Core study	Subsequent research/theory
Murder of Kitty Genovese Lab experiments by Darley and Latané (1968) Theory of diffusion of responsibility	Piliavin et al. (subway Samaritans)	Arousal cost–reward model
Haney et al. Prison simulation study	Reicher and Haslam (prison study) Social identity theory	
Features of autism Theory of mind Baron-Cohen et al. (1985) 'Sally-Anne' experiment	Baron-Cohen et al. (autism eyes) (1997)	Baron-Cohen et al. (autism eyes) (2001)

(4) What are the key terms (the jargon)?

One of the most difficult things when starting psychology is learning the jargon involved. You will find the same thing with any new subject that you start at A-level. It is worth persevering because after a few weeks you will be speaking like a true psychologist, and your non-psychology friends won't have a clue what you are talking about. Each core study has some jargon, and the ten most important terms for each are listed in the table below:

Core study	Ten key terms
Loftus and Palmer (eyewitness testimony)	eyewitness testimony; leading questions; memory reconstruction; car accident; speed estimates; smashed/collided/bumped/hit/contacted; broken glass; response-bias; original memory; after-the-fact memory
Baron-Cohen et al. (autism eyes)	autism; Asperger's syndrome; Tourette's syndrome; theory of mind; reading the mind in the eyes (eyes test); matched adults; DSM-IV and ICD-10; intelligence tests (WAIS-R); validity; strange stories
Savage-Rumbaugh (pygmy chimps)	language acquisition; *Pan paniscus* (pygmy chimpanzee); Kanzi and Mulika; Pan troglodytes; Sherman and Austin; longitudinal case study; lexigram; symbol acquisition and usage; vocabulary acquisition criterion; spontaneous, imitative and structured utterances
Samuel and Bryant (conservation)	cognitive development; conservation; fixed-array control; one-judgement task; pre-transformational question; post-transformational question; standard (Piagetian) task; pre-operational stage; operational stage; mean number of errors
Bandura et al. (bashing Bobo)	behaviourism; Bobo doll; imitative aggression; modelling; non-imitative aggression; observation; same-sex model; social learning; inter-rater reliability; aggressive gun play
Freud (Little Hans)	psychodynamic perspective; castration anxiety; two giraffe fantasy; Oedipus complex; phobia; widdler (penis); lumf (faeces); case study; phallic stage; unconscious mind
Maguire et al. (taxi-drivers)	London taxi-driver; 'The Knowledge'; navigational skills; structural MRI; VBM (voxel-based morphometry); ICV (intercranial volume); pixel counting; anterior hippocampus; posterior hippocampus; spatial representation
Dement and Kleitman (sleep and dreaming)	sleep cycles; REM (rapid eye movement); N-REM (non-rapid eye movement); EEG (electroencephalogram); dream recall; subjective dream duration estimates; eye movement patterns; throwing tomatoes; sleep laboratory experiment; doorbell and microphone
Sperry (split brain)	epilepsy; corpus callosum; commissurotomy; split-brain; left visual field; right visual field; left hemisphere and right hemisphere; left hand and right hand; lateralisation of function; key and case
Milgram (obedience)	obedience; authority; learning and memory; deception; shock generator; prods; right to withdraw; extreme tension; danger: severe shock; 450 volts
Reicher and Haslam (prison study)	Stanford prison experiment; prisoners and guards; pathological prisoner syndrome; pathology of power; tyranny; social identity theory; BBC prison study; experimental case study; ethics; rejecting and embracing inequality
Piliavin et al. (subway Samaritans)	adjacent area; critical area; altruism; arousal–cost–reward model; bystanders; diffusion of responsibility; pluralistic ignorance; victim; field experiment; model

Core study	Ten key terms
Rosenhan (sane in insane places)	schizophrenia; depersonalisation; participant observation; existential crisis; powerlessness; pseudo-patients; sane and insane; stickiness of psychodiagnostic labels; type one error (false positive); type two error (false negative)
Griffiths (fruit-machine gambling)	cognitive psychology; fruit machine; normative decision theory; heuristics and biases; regular and non-regular gamblers; thinking-aloud method; subjective (self-report) measures; rational and irrational verbalisations; flexible attributes and erroneous perceptions; skill variables
Thigpen and Cleckley (multiple personality)	multiple personality disorder; blackouts/amnesia; Black and White; hypnosis; Rorschach (ink-blot) test; psychometrics; IQ test; EEG; the letter; longitudinal study.

(5) What methods are used in the studies?

One of the most difficult things in psychology is measuring behaviour and experience accurately and it is important, therefore, to know how psychologists have tried to obtain their data. For example, if you want to measure aggression during fruit-machine gambling, you could:

- observe people and count the number of violent acts they commit
- interview people, getting them to talk out loud while they gamble
- measure their physiological changes

Each method of measurement produces a different result, so it is important to know which method is being used. You need to know not only the method that each study used, but also some detail about that method, including its advantages and disadvantages and the type of data that it produces. You need to know this for questions set in the Core Studies examination, but also for the Psychological Investigations (Unit G541) examination. For the Psychological Investigations paper you have to know about self-reports, experiments, observations and correlations. If you can link up each method with the core studies, you will not duplicate learning.

There are also several variations on each method, which can make matters more complicated. An observation may be naturalistic, i.e. where the participants do not know that they are being observed — for example, in the studies by Rosenhan and Piliavin et al. However, observations can also be controlled, whereby an environment is manipulated to include or exclude certain features and the participants know that they are being observed, as in the Reicher and Haslam prison study. Or there may be a controlled environment where the participants are unaware they are being observed, as in the Bandura et al. study, in which participants were observed through a one-way mirror.

An experiment may also be carried out in several ways. A laboratory experiment has a highly controlled environment and participants know that they are taking part in a study (e.g. the Dement and Kleitman sleep study). Alternatively, a field experiment may include some control, but the participants may not know that they are participating (e.g. the Piliavin et al. study). Thus, the method of the Piliavin et al. study was a field experiment, but data were gathered through observation.

Ecological validity concerns how true to real life a study is. If participants perform an artificial task in an experiment, the study is said to be low in ecological validity because this is not something they do in real life. Being in a laboratory is also low in ecological validity. Alternatively, if the natural, real-life, everyday behaviour of participants is observed, then this is high in ecological validity.

(6) Who were the participants, and how were they recruited?

Who the participants are, and how they are recruited, can affect the outcome of a study and the conclusions that can be drawn — not least of which is the issue of **generalisation** (although this is not included in the OCR specification). Many studies use participants who are **restricted** in some way (another issue not on the specification). For example, participants may be all students (as in the Loftus and Palmer study), or they may be all male (as in the Maguire et al. study). They may have been paid for participating (as in the Milgram study).

How participants are recruited is also important. If participants respond to a newspaper advertisement (as in the Reicher and Haslam study) then they are 'volunteers', and they may behave in ways that are different from those who do not or would never volunteer. In some studies the participants do not even know that they are taking part (as in the Rosenhan study). So, for each study, you should be able to identify the sampling technique (linked to what you know from psychological investigations), know how the participants were recruited and other relevant details such as how many took part, and be aware of at least one limitation of the sampling method.

(7) Does the study contravene any ethical guidelines?

The answer is almost certainly 'yes'. Many studies contravene the ethical guidelines laid down by the BPS (British Psychological Society) and the APA (American Psychological Association). A common question asked by students is whether *any* study is ethical. Here we consider all the ethical issues that may apply to each study:

- **Informed consent.** In the Milgram study, the participants thought they were taking part in a study on learning and memory, not obedience to authority.
- **Deception.** In the Piliavin et al. study, participants were deceived because they thought the victim was genuinely ill or drunk, whereas the male stooge (or confederate) was acting.
- **Harm.** This could be physical harm or psychological harm. This may occur if animals are studied (e.g. the Savage-Rumbaugh study) or if the participants are exposed to aggression, as in the Bandura et al. study.
- **Right to withdraw.** This cannot be granted if the participants do not know that they are being studied (e.g. Rosenhan study) or when, as in the Milgram study, the right to withdraw was denied as part of the actual study.
- **Debriefing.** This can happen in most studies, but is it possible if the participants are children or animals?

- **Confidentiality.** No participant is ever named or can be identified in the research, so this guideline is always met. Of course, participants can reveal themselves (e.g. Christine Sizemore, who was studied by Thigpen and Cleckley).

(8) How were the data collected?
There are many issues here:
- where a study was carried out
- what the participants in the study were asked to do
- how the researchers recorded their data

The method may be an experiment, but data can be gathered in many different ways. Data can appear as response categories (e.g. a tally chart), such as in the Bandura et al. and Piliavin et al. studies, but they can also be in the form of numbers, or what people say. This introduces two sets of issues that are outlined below.

Data in the form of numbers are known as **quantitative data**. These are data that are based on numbers and frequencies rather than on meaning or experience. **Qualitative data** describe meaning and experience rather than providing numerical values for behaviour. So which is better? Each has its advantages and disadvantages, and you could be asked an examination question about them. You should know whether a study gathers qualitative or quantitative data, or both.

The second issue concerns the time period over which data are gathered. Data may be collected over a short period, perhaps a few minutes. This is known as **snapshot** data because, in the context of an entire lifetime, a few minutes in a study provides merely a snapshot of a person's behaviour and experience. Alternatively, data may be gathered over a longer period, perhaps days, months or years. This is known as **longitudinal** data. You should know whether a study gathers snapshot or longitudinal data.

(9) What are the results of the study? What conclusions can be drawn?
Once the data have been gathered, we need to know what they mean. If we accept the data as valid, how can we summarise what has been found? If we go back to the original aims of the study, what do the results tell us? For example, Milgram's obedience study reveals something about the conditions under which people perform barbaric acts.

Sometimes it is possible to explain the same data in more than one way. Watch any political programme to see how statistics can be used to prove that the economy is booming (or not). On this course you will become more sceptical about data, and you will learn to interpret them better. Some of the studies also have implications for how we might like to change the way that we live or how we make sense of the world.

(10) Methodological issues (reliability and validity)
The OCR specification requires you to know about reliability and validity. Although you will cover other methodological issues as part of the course, in the examination you should only find specific questions on reliability and validity.

Reliability is how consistent something is. If your car always starts first time (or indeed never starts first time), you can describe it as reliable. If it sometimes starts and sometimes does not, it is unreliable. In psychology, the reliability of a psychological measuring device (e.g. a test or scale) is the extent to which it gives consistent measurements. If the consistency of measurement is high, so is the reliability of the tool.

Validity is concerned with whether an experiment or procedure for collecting data actually measures or tests what it claims to measure or test.

If I devised an intelligence test, how would I know whether it was accurately measuring intelligence? How would I know if my test is valid? If a person scored an IQ of 120 on my test and an IQ of 120 on an existing test, then because the existing test measures intelligence, so must my test. I conclude that my test is valid.

There are always other methodological issues involved in any study. For example, in experiments, in order to make sure that the manipulation of the independent variable is *causing* the change in the dependent variable, it is important for the researcher to *control* any **confounding variables**. Confounding variables are factors other than the independent variable that may affect the dependent variable.

(11) Strengths and limitations of the studies
The OCR specification requires you to provide some evaluative comment about the studies. You should remember that evaluation can be positive (a strength) or negative (a weakness, limitation or criticism). For more details on evaluation, see p. 41.

A good starting point is to consider the method. What are the strengths and limitations of the method used? Was the study ethical? Was it low in ecological validity? Was the sample representative? Were the findings of the study useful? Can the findings be generalised? You can apply these questions to every study, as well as the other evaluative points that apply specifically to each study.

(12) Similarities to and differences from other studies
An examination question could ask you for one similarity and one difference between two studies. This may appear to be daunting, since there are 15 studies and many aspects to each study. However, as you go through the course you will realise that there are many links between the studies:
- How many are based in a laboratory?
- How many involve observation?
- How many involve deception?
- How many use qualitative data?

You could list all the possible methods (laboratory experiment, field experiment, observation, self-report etc.) and when you have dealt with a study, simply add it to your list. Remember that some studies involve more than one method. The Piliavin et al. study is a field experiment, but it also involves observation. So you could create another list of all the issues that you need to know about:
- snapshot and longitudinal
- qualitative and quantitative

- high and low ecological validity
- ethics (subdivided into different guidelines)

Again, as you look at each study indicate their features in a table like the one below:.

	Experiment (lab)	Experiment (field)	Observation	Snapshot	Longitudinal	Qualitative	Quantitative
Milgram	Yes	No	No	Yes	No	No	Yes
Piliavin et al.	No	Yes	Yes	Yes	No	No	Yes
Bandura et al.	Yes	No	Yes	Yes	No	No	Yes
Freud	No	No	No	No	Yes	Yes	No

(13) Alternative methodologies and 'What if?'

Everyone asks 'What if?' questions and imagines how their life might change if things had been different. Section B questions always ask you to 'Suggest two changes to your chosen study', and following this you will have to think about the effect that the changes may have on the results. For example, what if the Milgram study had been entirely ethical? I imagine that every participant would believe that there was no point to the study and would not press any buttons on the shock generator. Milgram would have had no results at all, and he would not have been able to draw conclusions about how people obey authority. But this is just my opinion; you may have different views — and that is precisely the point of this question. There is no right or wrong answer here, just a question to make you think about changes and to explain your thoughts. Here are some 'What if?' suggestions.

What if the sample was different?

Many studies were carried out on student samples, or on participants who were paid. Many studies used only males. What would happen if a different group of people had been selected?

What if the location was different?

Many studies are carried out in laboratories, but real-life behaviour occurs outside these locations. What if you repeated a laboratory experiment in a different location? What if the study was more ecologically valid? If you think that you would get a different result, why is this, and what does it tell us about the psychological research?

What if the procedure was different?

If you changed the way that the study was carried out, how would the results change?

What if the procedure was ethical?

What if participants had fully informed consent (for example, they were told 'this is a study on obedience to authority')? What if there were no deceptions ('this shock generator is not actually giving any shocks to the learner, who is actually a part-time actor')? Think about how these changes would affect the results.

What if the method or nature of the data was changed?

What if you completely changed the method used to gather data? Instead of a laboratory experiment, what if a self-report questionnaire was used? What if qualitative data were gathered instead of quantitative data?

It is important to summarise the studies, because it is good revision technique and it reminds you what you are writing about. Consider two alternatives: one should always be a different method. For the Loftus and Palmer study, what if it was repeated with a real car crash? The other alternative should be an issue, and this could be different for each study. For example, for the Milgram study, you could consider making the study ethical, and for the Reicher and Haslam study you could propose repeating the study with female participants. Always consider what effect this would have on the results. If you complete each section of this table after each study is taught, the study will be fresh in your mind and you will then have a ready-made revision table at the end of the course. The following table is completed for one study, but you can expand it to include all the studies.

	Piliavin et al. (subway Samaritans)
Summary	Study into bystander behaviour. Ill or drunk victim on train. Observers record quantitative data of speed of helping etc.
Alternative 1: different method	Self-report questionnaire gathering quantitative data. Ask people at a station what they would do if a person who was ill fell over. Would they help or not? Gathering qualitative data rather than quantitative
Effect	I think that 100% of people would say they would help. They would give socially desirable answers. In the actual study, 62 out of 65 participants helped, and, using this method, I think the figure would be 65 out of 65. The overall conclusion would be the same
Alternative 2: ethical	If the study was repeated in a real train, but was made ethical, then people would be told that the victim would pretend to be ill or drunk, and that their behaviour would be observed. This would make the study ethical in terms of informed consent and deception
Effect	When the victim falls over, no one would help, because each passenger would know that he or she was pretending. The model would then come in to help, and a passenger would probably say that there was no point in helping because everything was faked. There would be no helping behaviour, and the results and conclusions would be very different

Content
Guidance

This section looks at the core approaches, perspectives, issues and methods in more detail. A consideration of each of these will allow you to explore some of the themes and debates that run through psychology, and provide you with essential information for essay writing and examinations, such as bullet-point strengths and weaknesses. There are also subsections on how to evaluate, assessment objectives and links to A2 study.

The core studies are divided into five core *approaches* of psychology. These are:

- **Cognitive**
- **Developmental**
- **Physiological**
- **Social**
- **Individual differences**

There are two *perspectives*:

- **Behavioural**
- **Psychodynamic**

There are four main *issues*:

- **Ethics**
- **Ecological validity**
- **Longitudinal and snapshot studies**
- **Qualitative data and quantitative data**

There are four main *methods*:

- **Experimental**
- **Case studies**
- **Self-reports**
- **Observations**

Core approaches of psychology
The cognitive approach

Cognitive psychology is about mental processes such as remembering, perceiving, understanding and producing language, solving problems, thinking and reasoning. It is an area of psychology that deals with abstract, invisible things that are not easy to pin down and define. Try asking yourself the question 'what is thought?' Then, when you have answered that, go on to the next question, 'where is thought?'

One of the central concerns of cognitive psychology is with the question of how information is processed by the brain. The ability to act in ways that are recognisably human depends upon the ability to make sense of the world in which we live.

The three areas of focus for OCR are memory, understanding and communication.

Memory

We take our memory for granted until it fails us. Then we experience all kinds of irritating phenomena, such as the feeling that the thing we want to recall is on the tip of our tongue but we cannot quite remember it. On other occasions, our memory will surprise us and we will recall unusual pieces of information or personal events for no obvious reason. The OCR specification focuses on just one aspect: where our memory plays tricks on us and we remember things that never happened. For example, do you have any memories of events where you can see yourself doing something? If, like many other people, you have 'memories' like this, it is obvious that they cannot be an accurate record of what you perceived at the time, because you could not have seen yourself. Your memory has made the event into a mental home movie and then sold it to you as a record of the event.

Loftus and Palmer's (1974) analysis of the accuracy of eyewitness testimony illustrates how cognitive psychology can be put to work in addressing important, real-life questions. People put a lot of faith in evidence supplied by eyewitnesses, both in the context of the courtroom and in the context of everyday conversations about events. The faulty memories of some of Loftus and Palmer's subjects suggest that the testimony of eyewitnesses should perhaps be regarded more sceptically.

Understanding

Another important issue in cognitive psychology concerns what we mean by the term **mind**. The remarkable thing about human beings is that we are able to reflect on our own experience and describe this experience to each other. One of the puzzles that emerges is that even when we know about how the brain works and we can describe our cognitive processes, we still cannot account for our unique personal experience of the world. We are all aware that we have a mind, but what is it and how does it work?

The study by Baron-Cohen et al. (1997) is about autistic children and tests the hypothesis that the central deficit of autism is a failure to develop a 'theory of mind'. In other words, the claim is that autistic children and adults are not very good at understanding what is going on in someone else's mind. The study tested for the theory of mind in adults using the 'reading the mind in the eyes' test, which involves viewing a photograph of a person's eyes and then choosing which words best describe the emotion that the person is experiencing. Read the study to find out what happens. You can even take the test for yourself.

Communication

Communication is a basic feature of all living things. Human beings love to communicate and devise all manner of ways to get messages from one person to another. We also communicate in a lot of unconscious ways, and pass messages about our intentions, our attitudes and our emotions. The basic ingredients of communication are a sender, a message and a receiver, though it is worth noting that the message the sender sends is often not the same as the message the receiver receives.

Human beings are arguably unique in possessing the ability to communicate with language, although this is challenged by Gardner and Gardner's study of Washoe, which is supported by Savage-Rumbaugh's study of Kanzi, a male pygmy-chimpanzee. Kanzi (and his younger sister Mulika) were taught to communicate using a 'visual symbol system' — basically a keyboard (or lexigram) with geometric shapes that lit up when touched, which was connected to a speech synthesiser, allowing the word to be heard. This was a longitudinal study, and assessment of communication ability was based on symbol acquisition and usage; the vocabulary acquisition criterion; and spontaneous, imitative and structured utterances. Whether Savage-Rumbaugh was successful in teaching Kanzi and Mulika is for you to decide when you read the article.

Questions about cognitive psychology

You could be asked a Section A (short-answer) question, such as:
- Give one assumption of the cognitive approach.
- Give one advantage of the cognitive approach.
- Give one criticism of the cognitive approach.

You could be asked a Section C (essay) question, such as:
- Outline one assumption of the cognitive approach in psychology.
- Describe how the cognitive approach could explain understanding/communication/memory processes.
- Describe one similarity and one difference between one named cognitive study and any other cognitive study (or any other named study).
- Discuss the strengths and limitations of the cognitive approach using examples from a named cognitive study (or studies).

The developmental approach

Developmental psychology is sometimes understandably, but misleadingly, thought of as child psychology: understandably, because the major part of the literature in developmental psychology is about children; misleadingly, because it gives the impression that psychological development stops as the child enters adulthood. A truly comprehensive developmental psychology should concern itself with the whole **lifespan** of human development. However, the OCR core studies focus exclusively on child development.

There are arguably three classic approaches in developmental psychology, which represent three very different traditions in psychology. They distinguish between **cognitive, affective** and **behavioural** features of human experience and behaviour: in other words, what we think (cognitive), how we feel (affective), and what we do (behavioural). In this section, studies that illustrate each approach have been selected.

Cognitive development

The most important theorist in the cognitive tradition is Jean Piaget, who became interested in how his own children developed their way of interpreting the world. One of Piaget's conclusions was that children under 7 years of age, in the pre-operational stage, think differently from children over 7 years of age, who are in the operational stage. He devised a number of conservation experiments to test this. Piaget's methodology has been criticised by Rose and Blank. They suggested that asking children questions twice was confusing for them, and thought that asking only one question would produce different findings. Samuel and Bryant (1984) compared the one-judgement task with the traditional Piagetian two-question task. They also compared children of different ages to examine Piaget's division at 7 years of age, and they looked at conservation tasks, using a range of different materials.

Affective development

The work of Freud gives us some insight into the emotional development of children. His theories were very influential on Western culture and social policy during the twentieth century. He proposed that each child goes through a number of stages of psychosexual development: beginning with the oral stage, followed by the anal stage, before moving into the third, phallic, stage. In the phallic stage, the Oedipus complex is central for boys, who use their mother to express the desires of the id. The case study chosen is about Little Hans, a boy who was in the phallic stage and going through the Oedipus complex. Freud's interpretations of events, such as the giraffe episode, illustrate the approach he took, and this core study will certainly provoke discussion in your class. Freud's approach developed into a whole school of thought — the psychodynamic perspective.

Behavioural development

The third classic approach, covering the behavioural aspects of human development, is provided by behaviourism. The influence of the behaviourists on psychology as a whole has been far-reaching, so it is essential to look at their work. Early behaviourists believed that all behaviour is learned, and Pavlov and Skinner coined the terms **classical** and **operant conditioning**. Bandura extended this research by looking at how children learn. He called his approach **social learning theory**, in the belief that children learn through observation and imitation. If behaviour is observed, it will be imitated; if behaviour is not observed, it will not be known by the child, and so it cannot be imitated or become part of the child's behaviour. To demonstrate that any behaviour could be learned, Bandura chose to look at the imitation of aggression in his 1961 study with Ross and Ross.

Questions about developmental psychology

You could be asked a Section A (short-answer) question, such as:
- Give one assumption of the developmental approach.
- Give one advantage of the developmental approach.
- Give one criticism of the developmental approach.

You could be asked a Section C (essay) question, such as:
- Outline one assumption of the developmental approach in psychology.
- Describe how the developmental approach could explain cognitive development.
- Describe one similarity and one difference between one named developmental study and any other developmental study (or any other named study).
- Discuss the strengths and limitations of the developmental approach, using examples from a named developmental study (or studies).

The physiological approach

Physiological psychology explores human behaviour and experience by looking at people as if they were biological machines.

This idea has some value because it is clear that our biology affects our behaviour and experience. On a simple level, we know that certain foodstuffs, such as coffee or alcohol, will affect the way we perceive the world and the way we behave. However, the question that arises is: how much does our biology affect us, and what other factors intervene to affect the response? Put another way, to what extent does our biology *determine* our behaviour (see 'Links to A2 study' on p. 45).

Some studies in physiological psychology look at the structure and function of the brain to determine which parts of it are responsible for particular actions. Other research looks at the interaction between our hormones and our thought processes (such as the displaced core study by Schachter and Singer).

content guidance

Methodology

Early physiological studies used rather cumbersome methods to investigate various physiological processes. For example, studies were performed in which electrodes were attached to the brains of animals and these areas were stimulated. This type of experimentation might sound barbaric, but we now know, for example, that specific areas of the hypothalamus are responsible for eating behaviour. In a totally different set of studies, it was discovered that the corpus callosum allows the two hemispheres of the brain to communicate with each other.

In 1968 Sperry performed a series of experiments on 'split-brain' patients who had had their corpus callosum severed, with fascinating results. He discovered that if an object was presented to the left visual field, the participants were unable to name it, but they could name the object if it was presented to the right visual field. So, it was concluded, not only is information from the right visual field processed by the left hemisphere (and vice versa), but the language function is located in the left hemisphere. More recently, new technology such as MRI and PET scanners has led to a significant increase in research to determine which parts of the human brain are related to specific functions. If radioactive glucose is injected into someone, it will travel throughout his or her body. Moreover, if it is metabolised (used by cells which are activated), it 'lights up' the scanner, and so a specific part of the body can be attributed to a specific function. This was done in a 1997 study by Maguire et al., one of the core studies, in which they discovered that in taxi-drivers the right hippocampus is used for navigation in large environments — specifically, when mentally recalling a London route. In the 2000 study by Maguire et al., it was discovered that the posterior hippocampi of taxi-drivers were significantly larger than those of control subjects.

Sleep

Why do we sleep? We still don't know, but we do know quite a lot about sleep cycles. Did you know that you have three to four dreams during every sleep period (even if you can't remember them all)? It is also known that we alternate between periods of REM (rapid eye movement, where our eyes actually move under our closed lids) and non-REM sleep. There are stages of non-REM sleep too, ranging from stage 1 (the lightest) to stage 4 (the deepest).

We progress through these stages after we fall asleep, then come out of stage 4 sleep and re-enter stages 3, 2 and 1. After this, we enter REM sleep, where we have a dream for a short time. We then drift down again into a deeper sleep. By the end of the sleep period we have had very little non-REM sleep and much more REM sleep. Dement and Kleitman, in their 1957 study, confirmed this, but added several interesting aspects. For example: do you think that you can estimate how long you have been dreaming? Their participants could. Do you think that the direction of your eye movements, under closed lids, reflects the actual content of your dream? They woke a participant whose eyes were moving horizontally and asked about the dream. The participant replied that he or she had been dreaming about two people throwing tomatoes at each other, and so the content of the dream matched the eye movement.

Questions about physiological psychology

You could be asked a Section A (short-answer) question, such as:
- Give one assumption of the physiological approach.
- Give one advantage of the physiological approach.
- Give one criticism of the physiological approach.

You could be asked a Section C (essay) question, such as:
- Outline one assumption of the physiological approach in psychology.
- Describe how the physiological approach could explain sleep and dreaming (or an aspect of another core study).
- Describe one similarity and one difference between one named physiological study and any other physiological study (or another named study).
- Discuss the strengths and limitations of the physiological approach, using examples from a named physiological study (or studies).

The social approach

Social psychology, as the label suggests, is concerned with the social side of human life. Social psychologists look at the numerous complex issues that surround human interaction and human relationships. They look at how the *individual* behaves rather than at how groups behave, and also at how that behaviour may be modified by social contexts that both frame and direct the individual's actions and experiences.

When we study social psychology, it is important to bear in mind that we are both the producers of, *and* the products of, the relationships, groups, cultures and societies to which we belong. Society moulds us, but we also mould society. In fact, one of the A2 debates (see 'Links to A2 study' on p. 45) is about how much importance to give to the individual or to the society in our explanations of social behaviour. In other words, when we are trying to understand why someone has done or said something, do we look to that person or do we look to the society for the causes of that action?

Social influence

We like to think that we are true to ourselves in what we do and say, and that we only follow everyone else when we want to. However, a number of social psychological investigations have suggested that we may be more susceptible to social influence than we think. The study by Milgram (1963), for example, shows the extent to which ordinary people are susceptible to following the demands of an authority figure, even when those demands require them to do something that is morally indefensible.

Milgram's results were shocking because no one predicted that the participants would obey the authority figure to such an extent. Obedience to authority was also studied by Hofling (1966), who found that nurses would ignore hospital policy and administer a lethal dose of a drug simply because they were told to — not in person, but by a 'doctor' at the other end of the telephone.

Social roles

We all play a variety of different **roles** in our lives, much like an actor on the stage. Any given person might be, say, a woman, a student, a mother, a daughter, a wife, a colleague, a friend, a squash partner, a neighbour and so on. All of these roles are played in relation to other people: to play the role of student there has to be a teacher; to be a hero there must be a villain.

Each role carries with it certain **rules** about how we must behave to fulfil the require-ments of that role. Students, for example, have to turn up at an agreed time on an agreed day for a psychology class. What if you were allocated the role of prison guard or prisoner? Would you adopt that role? The Stanford Prison Experiment by Haney et al. (1973) showed the powerful effect that roles can have on people's behaviour. Zimbardo concluded that 'guard aggression...was emitted as a "natural" consequence', and this supports the **banality of evil thesis**. Zimbardo's explanation of the parti-cipants' behaviour has been questioned, although he still defends it in what he calls the Lucifer effect. Reicher and Haslam (2006) re-think the **psychology of tyranny** and the banality of evil thesis. They believe that there is no evidence, either histor-ical or psychological, that people naturally adopt a role (or blindly follow orders). They argue, and their thesis is supported by their BBC prison study, that the evidence supports an interactionist thesis, i.e. that taking on a tyrannical role is an active choice.

Bystander apathy

Social behaviour can either be pro-social or anti-social. In the early 1960s, Kitty Genovese was murdered on her way home, and although there were 38 witnesses to the killing, no one called the police. However, the recent re-examination of this event by Manning et al. questions the original claims (about the number of witnesses and that the witnesses remained inactive). The lack of response was labelled as bystander apathy, and this led to many laboratory experiments being conducted, especially by Darley and Latané, who explained it in terms of **diffusion of responsibility**. In their studies, such as the one called 'a lady in distress', they found that when people were in a group, no one helped, as no one person was specifically responsible. The exper-iment by Piliavin et al. (1969) examined the way in which people behaved in a real-life setting (on a subway train in New York) rather than in a laboratory. They found that most people helped spontaneously, disproving the diffusion of responsibility hypothesis.

Questions about social psychology

You could be asked a Section A (short-answer) question, such as:

- Give one assumption of the social approach.
- Give one advantage of the social approach.
- Give one criticism of the social approach.

You could be asked a Section C (essay) question, such as:

- Outline one assumption of the social approach in psychology.
- Describe how the social approach could explain obedience (or an aspect of another core study).
- Describe one similarity and one difference between one named social study and any other social study (or another named study).
- Discuss the strengths and limitations of the social approach, using examples from a named social study (or studies).

Individual differences

Psychology often makes *generalisations* about people, such as how people behave, think and feel. Although some of these general statements are quite useful, they ignore the *differences* between groups of people, and between individual people. Generalisations apply to most people for most of the time, but they do not apply to everyone all of the time. For example, if we wanted to talk about human aggression, we might be able to say something about how all people show their aggression, but we would have to acknowledge the differences that exist. Some groups of people are much more aggressive than others: for example, men are, on the whole, more aggressive than women, and army commandos are, on the whole, more aggressive than Buddhists. These are examples of groups that have different levels and styles of aggression. Within those groups there will also be some individual differences. You might know some women who are very aggressive and some men who are non-aggressive. The problem for psychology is to identify the features that we *share* with other people and still acknowledge the *differences* between individuals.

Much of the psychology that is taught in British and North American universities and colleges is fairly insensitive to cultural differences. However, the different cultures that exist within our societies, and around the world, do not share the same behaviours and social structures. It is important to bear this in mind when you read any psychology book.

Abnormality

An issue that comes under the heading of individual differences is what psychologists refer to as abnormality. Some people have very unusual thoughts and feelings, or display some unusual behaviour patterns. Sometimes we regard this as eccentricity, and other times we view it as a sign of mental ill-health. The judgement to make is whether someone is just being different or whether he or she is being odd. The way we make this distinction is influenced by a range of factors, including our culture, class, religion and general outlook on life.

Psychological diagnosis of abnormality is an attempt to classify oddness in people. It is a difficult process that is steeped in controversy. Observers often cannot agree on a diagnosis for a patient, and classifying a person can lead to the carers ignoring signs and symptoms that do not fall into the diagnostic pattern. Despite these problems, diagnosis is attempted because it has some benefits — one of which should be effective treatment.

This section contains two studies that look at the issues around abnormality and its treatment. The study by Rosenhan (1973) challenges the ability of professional workers to distinguish the sane from the insane. The study by Thigpen and Cleckley (1954) describes the famous case of a young woman with multiple personality disorder. This study still causes some controversy among professional workers, although it captured the public imagination through the film *The Three Faces of Eve*.

Gambling behaviour

Another abnormality is compulsive gambling. This is an impulse-control disorder, and is categorised alongside kleptomania and pyromania in the DSM-IV (the handbook that lists all mental disorders).

It is estimated that 1% of the UK population are problem gamblers. Many theories and explanations have been proposed, but the area is complex because gambling is multi-faceted, meaning that there is no single explanation that can explain all of its aspects. Mark Griffiths is one of the world's leading experts on gambling, and his publication of well over 2,000 papers illustrates the complexity of the problem. One area of study is fruit-machine gambling.

In the 1994 study (the OCR core study), he asked participants to 'think aloud' when they were playing on fruit machines, finding, for example, that gamblers make more irrational verbalisations — such as 'the machine likes me' — than non-gamblers.

Questions about individual differences

You could be asked a Section A (short-answer) question such as:
- Give one assumption of the individual differences approach.
- Give one advantage of the individual differences approach.
- Give one criticism of the individual differences approach.

You could be asked a Section C (essay) question, such as:
- Outline one assumption of the individual differences approach in psychology.
- Describe how the individual differences approach could explain gambling behaviour (or an aspect of another core study).
- Describe one similarity and one difference between one named individual differences study and any other individual differences study (or another named study).
- Discuss the strengths and limitations of the individual differences approach, using examples from a named individual differences study (or studies).

Core perspectives in psychology

There are a number of perspectives in psychology: two are introduced at AS, and others may appear at A2 depending on the options chosen. For example, the 'Psychology and Education' option introduces humanistic theories of motivation. At AS the two perspectives are behaviourist and psychodynamic.

The psychodynamic perspective

The psychodynamic perspective is based on the work of Freud and emphasises the role of the unconscious mind: the id, ego and superego, and the influence that child-hood experiences have on our future lives. Freud proposed a number of psychosexual stages through which each child passes, emphasising the Oedipus complex in the phallic stage. On top of this, Freud developed a method of psychotherapy that he called psychoanalysis (literally 'analysis of the psyche'). This was based on an under-standing of the mind through interpretive methods, introspection and clinical obser-vations. His approach has been criticised for its lack of objectivity, but Freud readily accepted this. The core study on Little Hans is a perfect illustration of Freud's beliefs and methods.

The behaviourist perspective

The behaviourist perspective takes the view that the subject matter of psychology should have standardised procedures, with an emphasis on the study of observable behaviour that can be measured objectively, rather than a focus on the mind or consciousness. Early behaviourists included Skinner, whose work involved pigeons and rats, and Watson, who claimed that all behaviour is learned and that he could take any 12 healthy infants and, by applying behavioural techniques, create whatever kind of person he desired. Bandura is also a behaviourist, and his early work in the 1960s dealt with observational learning and modelling. He applied these principles to aggression and devised the Bobo doll experiment — the core study that is used to introduce you to the behaviourist perspective.

Questions about perspectives

You could be asked a Section A (short-answer) question, such as:

- Give one assumption of the psychodynamic/behaviourist perspective.
- Give one strength of the psychodynamic/behaviourist perspective.
- Give one criticism of the psychodynamic/behaviourist perspective.

You could be asked a Section C (essay) question, such as:
- Outline one assumption of the psychodynamic/behaviourist perspective.
- Describe how the psychodynamic/behaviourist perspective could explain gambling behaviour (or an aspect of another core study).
- Discuss the strengths and limitations of the psychodynamic/behaviourist perspective, using examples from a named individual differences study (or studies).

Core issues in psychology

There are many issues to debate in psychology, but for AS the OCR specification focuses on just four. These are **ethics**, **ecological validity**, **longitudinal and snapshot studies**, and **qualitative and quantitative** data. What follows for each of the core issues is a definition; examples from core studies; and discussion points for essays. You could create revision guides based on the information that follows. You could also create a table like the following one and then add examples from all 15 studies. Note that the advantages and disadvantages are not exhaustive, and others should be added as you go through the course.

	Issue:
Description of issue	
Examples of core studies	1. 2. 3.
Strengths	1. 2. 3.
Weaknesses	1. 2. 3.

Ethics

Description

Ethics are a set of rules designed to distinguish between right and wrong. The British Psychological Society (BPS) and American Psychological Association (APA) have guidelines on consent, deception, the right to withdraw, harm, debriefing, confidentiality, the use of children, and the use of animals.

Examples

All 15 studies could go here. Some break more ethical guidelines than others, but it is also worth considering which ethical guidelines are *not* broken. For example, does any study breach the confidentiality of the participants?

Reasons for being unethical

- It may simulate a realistic situation.
- The ends may justify the means, i.e. what was learned was too important to dismiss it as unethical.

Reasons for being ethical

- Something may go seriously wrong; the participants may be harmed for life.
- Unethical studies may discourage future participation in psychological research. This may well lower the status of psychology; newspapers may label it as a 'crackpot' subject.

Ecological validity

Description

Ecological validity refers to how true a study is to real life. If a study is close to real life, we say that it is high in ecological validity and we can generalise. This means that we say it applies to most people most of the time. However, studies with low ecological validity cannot be used to generalise. Experiments low in ecological validity may be of limited value in psychology. Ecological validity can relate to the task that participants are required to do, and it can relate to the location of the study.

Examples

Which core studies are high in, and which are low in, ecological validity?
- High: Griffiths, Reicher and Haslam, Piliavin et al., Rosenhan
- Low: Loftus and Palmer, Bandura et al., Maguire et al.

Advantages of high ecological validity

- The study is located in a real-life setting, and so participants are more likely to behave 'normally'. There are less likely to be demand characteristics, meaning that, since the participant is not conscious of being studied, there will be no pressure on him/her to perform in a certain way.
- If a study is based on real life, it is more likely that strong generalisations can be made.

Problems in trying to achieve high ecological validity

- There may be a lack of control over confounding variables. Experimenters cannot control all variables; they may not be able to isolate one variable from many others.
- If a study is conducted in a natural environment, the experimenter may not have obtained the participants' consent, so the study would be unethical.
- It may be impossible, on a practical level, to create a real-life situation or make something happen naturally.
- The data are less reliable, i.e. if the study is repeated, entirely different data might be produced.

Longitudinal and snapshot studies

Description

A longitudinal study is one that monitors changes occurring over a period of time. A snapshot study is where data are gathered in a short period of time, perhaps a few minutes.

Examples

Which core studies are longitudinal and which are snapshot?
- Longitudinal: Freud, Thigpen and Cleckley, Savage-Rumbaugh
- Snapshot: Maguire et al., Griffiths, Milgram, Bandura et al., and many others

Strengths of longitudinal studies

- The development of specific individual(s) is tracked. A baseline is recorded at the start, and changes that occur over time (e.g. 5 years) in attitudes and behaviour can be measured.
- Studying the same participant means that individual differences such as intelligence are controlled.
- The effects of ageing can be seen, which makes this approach perfect for studying development, both within childhood and beyond.
- The long-term effects of a disorder or treatment, or exposure to a particular situation can be observed.

Weaknesses of longitudinal studies

- Over time, participants may drop out of the study. This is known as participant attrition.
- Once started, the study cannot be changed or new variables introduced.
- The researchers may become attached to the participants. Bias may be introduced, and the study can become less objective.

Strengths of snapshot studies

- They are a quick way to collect data, especially if long-term development is not relevant.
- They can be good for obtaining preliminary evidence before committing to expensive and time-consuming longitudinal work.
- They may give an indication of how people are likely to respond/behave.
- The data are likely to be quantitative, so statistical analysis is possible.

Weaknesses of snapshot studies

- It is not possible to study how behaviour may change over time (development), and one cannot see the long-term effectiveness or impact of a treatment/exposure to certain stimuli.
- The behaviour recorded is limited to that time, in that place and that culture.
- The data are likely to be quantitative (numbers), and the explanation as to why a participant behaved in a particular way will not be known.
- One cannot see the effects of societal changes on participants.

Qualitative and quantitative data

Description

Quantitative data are data that focus on numbers and frequencies rather than on meaning or experience. **Qualitative data** are data that describe meaning and experience rather than providing numerical values for behaviour.

Examples

Which core studies have quantitative elements, which have qualitative elements, and which have both?
- Qualitative: Freud, Thigpen and Cleckley
- Quantitative: Loftus and Palmer, Piliavin et al., Samuel and Bryant, Maguire et al.
- Both: Dement and Kleitman, Reicher and Haslam, Griffiths

Strengths of quantitative data

- Quantitative data allow statistics to be applied and comparisons to be made easily.
- Data are 'objective' and more 'scientific'.

Weaknesses of quantitative data

- Numbers are often produced without interpretation, possibly via a 'snapshot' study.
- People may be seen as nothing more than numbers in a reductionist approach.
- The data ignore any subjective element — the reason *why* a behaviour occurred.

Strengths of qualitative data

- The data can be in-depth, rich in detail, insightful and therefore not reductionist.
- The data can help us to understand why people behave in a particular way.

Weaknesses of qualitative data

- There may be problems of interpretation. Words and descriptions are more subjective than numbers, and are more open to bias and misinterpretation by participants.
- It may be much more difficult to make statistical comparisons.
- The data may be more prone to researcher bias, as information that best fits the researcher's hypothesis could be selected.
- The participants may give socially desirable answers. Participants may want to look good for the researcher.

Core methods in psychology

The OCR specification lists four different methods: experimental (divided into laboratory and field), case-study, self-report, and observation. Additionally, a number of methodological issues are raised, including reliability and validity.

Experimental method

Description

Laboratory experiment: a form of research in which variables are manipulated in order to discover cause and effect. It is commonly performed in a laboratory.

Field experiment: a study that follows the logic of an experiment, but is conducted in the outside world rather than the laboratory.

Natural experiment (also called a 'quasi-experiment'): an event in which variables change as a result of natural, political, social or economic circumstances, such that the outcome of these changes can then be studied.

Examples

Which core studies follow the experimental method?
- Laboratory: Loftus and Palmer, Samuel and Bryant, Bandura et al.
- Field: Griffiths, Piliavin et al.
- Natural: Baron-Cohen et al., Maguire et al.

Strengths of the experimental method

- Manipulation of one variable and control of confounding variables means that it is more likely to discover cause and effect.
- It is possible to control many confounding variables.
- The laboratory setting should ease the process of data collection, e.g. the use of a one-way mirror, electroencephalography (EEG) etc.
- As the study is in a laboratory, participants will have given consent, which may make the study more ethical.

Weaknesses of the experimental method

- Controlling variables is reductionist, as it is unlikely that any behaviour exists in isolation from other behaviours.
- The task performed is unlikely to be true to real life; the setting itself is low in ecological validity.
- The participants know they are taking part in a study, and may respond to demand characteristics (pressure to perform in a certain way because of the demands of the situation).

Case studies

Description

These involve a detailed description of a particular individual or group under study or treatment.

Examples

Freud, Thigpen and Cleckley, Sperry

Strengths of case studies

- The data gathered are rich and detailed.
- Participants are often studied over a period of time, so developmental changes can be recorded. This is longitudinal, and it often means that the data gathered are detailed.
- They are ecologically valid because the participant may well be studied as part of his or her everyday life.
- Rare or unique behaviours can be studied in detail.
- The sample *may* be self-selecting, which means that the participants are not chosen by the researchers.

Weaknesses of case studies

- There may be only one participant (or very few) involved, and so any conclusions cannot be generalised to other people.

- The participant may be unique and possibly 'not normal' in some way. This may mean that the researchers may not know how to proceed, and they may draw false conclusions.
- The researchers may become emotionally attached to the participant if only one person is studied over a period of time.

Self-reports

Description

Self-reports involve research that uses the participants' own account of their behaviour or experience.

Self-report methods include questionnaires, interviews, thinking aloud and diary methods.

Examples

Freud, Thigpen and Cleckley, Dement and Kleitman, Reicher and Haslam, Griffiths

Strengths of self-reports

- The participants are given the opportunity to express their feelings and explain their behaviour.
- The quality and richness of the data gained often outweighs any weaknesses.
- The participants may be less likely to drop out of the study if they are 'more than a number'.

Weaknesses of self-reports

- The data may be unique and not comparable with others.
- The participants may provide socially desirable responses/respond to demand characteristics.

Observations

Description

In its broadest sense, this is the core of psychological research. It is not just 'observational studies' that are based on 'observing'. On the contrary, all empirical work is, by definition, grounded in the act of observation. Experimenters observe the behaviour of their subjects, discourse analysts observe the texts with which they are working, interviewers observe the spoken responses of their subjects, and so on. Observations can be natural (as in the Piliavin et al. study), they can be controlled (as in the Bandura et al. study), or a participant can be an observer (as in the Rosenhan study).

Examples

Rosenhan, Piliavin et al., Bandura et al., Savage-Rumbaugh, Thigpen and Cleckley

Advantages of observation

- The observed behaviour is natural and can be measured objectively.
- The data are often quantitative, involving response categories.
- The participants may be unaware of the observation, and so are unaffected by the demand characteristics.

Disadvantages of observation

- The participants cannot explain why they behaved in particular way.
- The observer's view may be obstructed and the observations may not be reliable. However, this can be resolved with inter-rater reliability.
- Observations in certain situations may not be replicable.

Methodology: terms and concepts

Reliability

Reliability indicates to what degree something is consistent. The reliability of a questionnaire, for example, can be checked in two main ways:

- **Test–re-test method:** this is a system for judging the reliability of a psychometric test or measurement. It involves administering the same test to the same person on two different occasions, such as intervals 3 weeks apart, and comparing the results. The results can then be correlated.
- **Split-half method:** this involves splitting the test into two and administering each half of the test to the same person. The scores from the two halves should be the same (but only if certain test items are balanced equally).

The reliability of an observation is called **inter-rater reliability**, i.e. the extent to which two independent observers (coders/raters) agree on the observations that they have made.

Validity

Validity is concerned with whether an experiment or procedure for collecting data actually measures or tests what it claims to measure or test. There are several types of validity:

- **Concurrent validity:** a method for assessing validity by comparing the measure with some other measure that has been taken at the same time, i.e. which is occurring concurrently.
- **Construct validity:** a method for assessing validity by seeing how the measure matches up with theoretical ideas about what it is supposed to be measuring.
- **Criterion validity:** a method for assessing validity by comparing the measure with some other measure. If the other measure is assessed at roughly the same time as the original one, then the type of criterion validity being applied is concurrent validity; if it is taken much later, then it is predictive validity.
- **Face validity:** the degree to which a test or measure appears superficially as though it probably measures what it is supposed to.
- **Predictive validity:** a method for assessing validity by seeing how well the test correlates with some other measure, which is assessed after the test has been taken.

Confounding variables

There are three types of confounding variables that need to be controlled: situational, experimenter and participant.

Situational variables

If a study is carried out in a noisy place, the participants may be distracted and not concentrate on the task (unless the study requires the place to be noisy). The solution to this is to conduct the study in a quiet environment. All participants should be studied in the same quiet environment.

Experimenter variables

The presence of the researcher may affect the outcome of the experiment. This can happen in two ways:

- The mere presence of the experimenter may lead to **demand characteristics**. This is where the participant responds to the experiment in some way in order to please (or upset) the experimenter. One way to control the demand characteristics is by using a **single-blind** design.
- An experimenter who wants to achieve a particular outcome may give different 'signals' to participants, leading to **experimenter bias**. He or she may smile if a participant is doing what is desired, or may encourage them if they are not. This can be controlled in two ways. First, by giving all participants the same **standardised instructions**, and second by using a **double-blind** design, in which not only is the participant unaware of the behaviour that is expected, but the experimenter also does not know whether the participant is in the experimental group or the control group.

Participant variables

These are individual differences between participants, such as the level of motivation or any other relevant factor where participants may differ. This can be partially resolved by considering how the participants will be selected to match the various conditions of the experiment.

The selection of participants is part of the **experimental design**. A **repeated measures design** is where the same participant performs in all conditions. However, this could create **order effects**. In the simplest case (a two-condition experiment), if all the subjects perform first under condition A and then under condition B, and they perform better under condition B, this could be due simply to the subjects having practised under condition A, and having improved by the time that they performed under condition B. (A practice effect is one kind of order effect.) Conversely, partici-pants may perform better under condition A because they are fatigued or bored by the time that they perform under condition B. **Counterbalancing** controls this confounding variable by alternating the order in which subjects perform under the conditions of an experiment.

If an **independent groups design** is used, where participants only perform under one condition, then this eliminates any order effects, but it reintroduces individual differences between participants. This can be controlled partially by using large numbers of participants, so that any difference is balanced out across the conditions of the study.

Other methodological terms

action research: a method of undertaking social research which acknowledges that the researcher's presence is likely to influence people's behaviour, and so incorpo-rates the researcher's involvement as a direct and deliberate part of the research.

correlation: a measure of how strongly two, or more, variables are related to each other.

correlation coefficient: a number between –1 and +1 that expresses how strong a correlation is. If this number is close to 0, there is no real connection between the two. If it is close to +1 there is a positive correlation: in other words, if one variable is large, the other will also tend to be large. If it is close to –1, there is a negative correlation: in other words, if one variable is large, the other will tend to be small.

diary method: a way of studying what human beings do in everyday life by asking them to note down specific items of information at regular intervals or on appropriate occasions.

discourse analysis: a method of studying human experience by analysing what people say to one another, and how they express themselves — both symbolically and behaviourally.

double-blind control: a form of experimental control that aims to avoid self-fulfilling prophecies, by ensuring that neither the subjects nor the experimenter who carries out the study are aware of the experimental hypothesis.

participant observation: a method of study in which the investigator joins in the social process being observed.

population: in the context of research methods in psychology, this refers to the total set of potential observations from which a sample is drawn.

projective test: a psychometric test that involves providing the person with ambiguous stimuli, and seeing what meanings he or she reads into them. The idea is that this will illustrate the concerns of the unconscious mind.

psychometric test: an instrument that has been developed for measuring mental characteristics. Psychological tests have been developed to measure a wide range of things, including creativity, job attitudes and skills, brain damage, and, of course, 'intelligence'.

random sample: a sample in which every person from the defined population has an equal chance of being chosen.

sample: the group of subjects used in a study. Sampling involves the selection of people, animals, plants or objects drawn from a population for the purposes of studying that population.

self-fulfilling prophecy: the idea that expectations about a person or group can become true, simply because they have been stated.

standardisation: (a) the process of making sure that the conditions of a psychological study or psychometric test are always identical; (b) the process of establishing how the results of a psychometric test will usually turn out in a given population, by drawing up sets of population norms; (c) the process of comparing a new psychometric test with older, more established measures of the same thing.

Evaluation

Evaluation can sometimes appear to be the more difficult part of any course, but it need not be. You may have heard your teacher talking about assessment objective (AO2) and you are unsure what it is. If you have an opinion and can justify it, then you can evaluate. If you say 'I think that's rubbish', it is abuse rather than evaluation. But if you say 'I think that it's rubbish because...' and add appropriate comment, then you are evaluating.

Evaluation also includes saying what is good and giving credit where it is due. After studying his work, you may have negative views about Freud, but he was certainly original and so he should receive credit for this at the very least. The OCR philosophy has been always to credit answers where students show that they can think. If a study has been performed in a laboratory, you do not need to study a textbook and conclude 'A. N. Other writes that the XXX study is low in ecological validity because it was performed in a laboratory'. You can conclude this for yourself.

Assessment objectives

You do not need to worry too much about the details of the assessment objectives. When the examiners set exam papers, they follow the specification guidelines and include a certain percentage of questions about each assessment objective. The wording of each question must make it clear which assessment objective is being assessed. For example, some questions ask you to describe, and other questions will ask you to evaluate. So, all you have to do is answer the questions that are set. The skills covered by each assessment objective are summarised below.

Assessment objective 1: knowledge and understanding

You should be able to:
- recognise, recall and show understanding of scientific knowledge
- select, organise and communicate relevant information in a variety of forms, including extended prose

AO1 assesses what you know about psychology and whether you understand what you know. Examination questions testing AO1 ask you to identify, outline or describe.

Assessment objective 2: application of knowledge and understanding

You should be able to:
- analyse and evaluate scientific knowledge when presenting arguments and ideas
- apply scientific knowledge to unfamiliar situations, including those related to issues
- assess the validity, reliability and credibility of scientific information
- bring together scientific knowledge from different areas of the subject and apply them

AO2 assesses your evaluation skills, and the examination questions ask you to discuss, compare/contrast or suggest.

Assessment objective 3: science in practice

You should be able to:

- demonstrate ethical, safe and skilful practical techniques, selecting appropriate qualitative and quantitative methods
- make, record and communicate reliable and valid observations and measurements with appropriate precision and accuracy through using primary and secondary sources
- analyse, interpret, explain and evaluate the methodology, results and impact of your own and others' experimental and investigative activities in a variety of ways

AO3 is usually reserved for psychological investigations where you do some practical work. However, a small percentage of AO3 is assessed in the Core Studies paper, so you will get one or two questions on methodology, such as evaluation of results.

There are a number of common themes that you could raise about every study: the issues, methods and approaches that we have already considered. You can create a revision table with all the core studies across the top and the issues down the side, as shown below.

	Piliavin et al.	Loftus and Palmer
What approach did this study use? Check the strengths and weaknesses of the approach.		
Approach	Social psychology	Cognitive psychology
What perspective did this study use (if one applies)?		
Perspective	Not applicable	Not applicable
What method did the study use? Check the strengths and weaknesses of the method.		
Methodology	Field experiment (with observation)	Laboratory experiment
Was the study ethical? Consider a range of ethical guidelines and check their strengths and weaknesses.		
Ethics	Unethical: no informed consent, lots of deception, no right to withdraw Ethical: confidentiality, harm	Ethical: informed consent, no deception, no harm, right to withdraw, confidentiality
Was the study true to real life? Check the strengths and weaknesses of high and low ecological validity.		
Ecological validity	Very high, as the study was conducted on a real train with real people, and someone could really be ill or drunk.	Low, as judgements were made on the basis of a film clip rather than a real accident.
Was the study a snapshot or was it longitudinal? Look at the advantages and disadvantages of both snapshot and longitudinal data.		

	Piliavin et al.	Loftus and Palmer
Longitudinal or snapshot?	Snapshot study. The train journey was only 7.5 minutes long.	Snapshot study. It was the time taken to watch the films and then answer the questions.
What types of data were gathered? Look at the advantages and disadvantages of both qualitative and quantitative data.		
Qualitative or quantitative?	Quantitative, as specific numbers are observed, e.g. 62/65 helped when someone appeared to be ill. No one asked the participants why they helped or did not help.	Quantitative, as for Experiment 1, the specific m.p.h. is recorded, e.g. 40.5 m.p.h. for the verb 'smashed', and in Experiment 2, 16 participants reported seeing broken glass in the smashed condition.
Are there any evaluative comments that apply that are not mentioned above?		
General evaluation	1. There were different numbers of trials in the 'ill' and 'drunk' conditions, as the victims did not like pretending to be drunk. 2. What if the same people travel on the same train at the same time each day?	1. Only 45 participants were used in Experiment 1, and only nine in each condition. 2. The order of the verbs may not apply universally. In the UK, 'hit' is worse than 'bumped'.
Are there any similarities and differences between studies? (You could do this by drawing arrows on the table to link boxes.)		
Comparisons and contrasts	What are the similarities and differences between this core study and any other core study?	What are the similarities and differences between this core study and any other core study?

References

Darley, J. M. and Latané, B. (1968) 'Bystander intervention in emergencies: diffusion of responsibility', *Journal of Personality and Social Psychology*, Vol. 8, pp. 377–83.

Gardner, R. and Gardner, B. (1969) 'Teaching sign language to a chimpanzee', *Science*, Vol. 165, pp. 664–72.

Hofling, C. K. (1966) 'An experimental study of nurse–physician relationships', *Journal of Nervous and Mental Disease*, Vol. 141, pp. 171–80.

Manning, R., Levine, M. and Collins, A. (2007) 'The Kitty Genovese murder and the social psychology of helping: the parable of the 38 witnesses', *American Psychologist*, Vol. 62, pp. 555–62.

Miller, G. A. (1969) 'Psychology as a means of promoting human welfare', *American Psychologist*, Vol. 24, pp. 1063–75.

Raine, A., Buchsbaum, M. and LaCasse, L. (1997) 'Brain abnormalities in murderers indicated by positron emission tomography', *Biological Psychiatry*, Vol. 42, No. 6, pp. 495–508.

Rose, S. A. and Blank, M. (1974) 'The potency of context in children's cognition: an illustration through conservation', *Child Development*, Vol. 45, pp. 499–502.

Tajfel, H. (1970) 'Experiments in intergroup discrimination', *Scientific American*, Vol. 233, pp. 96–102.

Links to A2 study

If A-level courses were truly synoptic, all examinations would be set at the end of a 2-year period and you could bring into your answer anything that you learned throughout the course. If you are taking AS examinations at the end of your first year, they are not fully synoptic. However, there is no reason why you cannot bring what you learn at AS into any A2 examination. It may be helpful to think about some of the A2 debates now, so that when you get questions on them at A2 you will have already thought about them using AS material.

The A2 course introduces a number of debates that are not covered at AS:
- determinism and free will
- reductionism and holism
- nature versus nurture
- ethnocentrism
- psychology as a science
- individual and situational explanations
- the usefulness of psychological research

Determinism and free will

Determinism is the view that we do not have much control over our behaviour or our destiny, but are controlled by factors such as our biology or genetics, or by the reinforcements we are given. We can, therefore, have biological determinism and environmental determinism. There is also climatological determinism — the view that the climate determines our behaviour (why do we have examinations in the middle of summer?). There is even architectural determinism, the view that architecture determines the way that we behave. For example, the design of a gambling casino (high or low ceiling) can have a significant effect on our behaviour inside the building.

The opposite of determinism is free-will, with possibilism and probabilism in between.

Reductionism and holism

Reductionism is the process of explaining complex psychological phenomena by reducing them to their component parts. This is the opposite of holism, where the total is more than the sum of the parts. A number of core studies are reductionist. The Maguire et al. study looks at the role of the hippocampus as the centre of spatial awareness. A previous core study by Raine et al. (1997) looked specifically at glucose metabolism in various cortical and sub-cortical brain structures. There are a number of advantages and disadvantages to being reductionist: in theory it is easier to study one aspect rather than several interacting aspects, and if one aspect is isolated and others controlled, then study is more objective/scientifically acceptable. However, individual components may be difficult to isolate, and if an isolated behaviour is studied in a laboratory, then the study may lack ecological validity.

Nature versus nurture

Nature in this sense refers to the part of us that is inherited and genetic, as distinct from **nurture**, which refers to all influences after our birth (i.e. experience). The 'modern' version of this debate considers what percentage is inherited and what is learned. The Bandura et al. study illustrates the nurture viewpoint when it shows how any behaviour can be learned through observational learning and imitation.

Ethnocentrism

The term comes from the word '*ethnos*', meaning 'nation' in modern Greek, and '*kentro*' meaning 'centre'. Specifically, this means that we are 'nation-centred', but psychologists often take it to mean much smaller social groupings. Thus, it refers to the belief that our own viewpoint, or the viewpoint of people like us, is superior to that of others, particularly people who are different in some way. A previous core study (by Tajfel, 1970) looked at in-group favouritism and out-group discrimination. This often leads us to believe that our ethnic group, nation, religion, or football team is superior to all others.

Psychology as a science

There is much evidence to support the view that psychology is a science. Any experiment is scientific and so are the quantitative data to which statistics are applied. A number of core studies adopt this methodology, but what about the other studies? It could be argued that psychology owes its richness to the many different methodologies that it uses. So asking people questions and gathering qualitative data may be less rigorous, but it is equally valuable to our understanding of behaviour and experience.

Individual and situational explanations

Individual and situational explanations refer to the way that we describe the cause of a behaviour as being due to something in that person (**individual** or **dispositional**) or as a response to the situation that they are in (**situational**). If you look back to the 'Social approach' section on pp. 26–28, you will see that we have already looked at this debate.

The usefulness of psychological research

This refers to the contribution that psychology makes to human welfare. Miller (1969) argued that psychology should aim to improve people's quality of life, and that it should be useful to everyone rather than representing a commercial opportunity for the few. There is a long-standing debate between the pure and applied branches of psychology. The OCR specification takes the applied route, particularly for A2, where real-life occupations are considered such as forensic and criminological psychology, and sport psychology. Not everything that psychologists study and claim is useful, but they often make the world a more interesting place in which to live.

Questions
&
Answers

The Core Studies examination paper G542 lasts 2 hours (see pp. 5–6), and the format is as follows:

- Section A: answer *all* of the questions.
- Section B: answer the *one* question.
- Section C: answer *one* question from a choice of two.

In the questions that follow, questions 1–6 are typical of questions from Section A. Question 7 is an example of a B-section question and question 8 is an example of a question from Section C.

Examiner's comments

All candidate responses are followed by examiner's comments. These are preceded by the icon *e* and indicate where credit is due. In the weaker answers, they also point out areas for improvement, specific problems and common errors such as lack of clarity, weak or non-existent development, irrelevance, misinterpretation of the question and mistaken meanings of terms.

Loftus and Palmer

(a) From the study by Loftus and Palmer (eyewitness testimony), briefly describe the sample of participants in experiment 1. (2 marks)

> As this is a 'two things for 2 marks' type of question, a very brief answer would suffice. This is an AO1 question, as it requires recall of knowledge.

(b) From the study by Loftus and Palmer (eyewitness testimony): give one problem with using a restricted sample of participants. (2 marks)

> The mark scheme requires candidates to provide an example of any logical problem, such as the inability to generalise to the wider population.
>
> 1 mark is allocated for a basic correct statement, and a second mark is awarded for elaboration of the statement. Giving an example of a problem is not part of the study, so candidates have to apply their *evaluative* skills. Therefore, this is an AO2 question.

■ ■ ■

Answer to question 1: candidate A

(a) 45 university students.

> There were indeed 45 participants in experiment 1, so 1 mark is awarded. The participants were also university students, and so a second mark is awarded. This answer scores a maximum 2 marks.

(b) A problem is that the findings cannot be used to represent a larger population.

> This answer is correct, as the candidate refers to the inability to generalise. However, it is worth only 1 mark, as there is no elaboration.

■ ■ ■

Answer to question 1: candidate B

(a) The study by Loftus and Palmer (eyewitness testimony) was split into two experiments. In the first experiment, a pool of 45 participants was drawn from a particular area, to watch driving-safety films and then to fill out a questionnaire on the film, the most critical question being the estimate of the speed of the car: 'how fast were the cars going when they smashed/hit/contacted/bumped/collided?'

> This candidate has written a very long answer, with too much detail. Everything that is written is correct, but the candidate discusses the *procedure* rather than the *participants*. If the response does not answer the question, then it scores no marks. However, the candidate does mention 45 participants, and that scores 1 mark. The candidate then writes that 'they are drawn from a particular area', but this is too

vague to be awarded a mark. *Note: you must answer the question set, and you must write an appropriate amount for the time available and the marks allocated.*

(b) The findings derived from a restricted sample of participants cannot be generalised to other groups of people from different places, cultures, educational and ethnic backgrounds. This is because of the limited number and type of people used in the study, which is from a small section of people in the overall population.

✍ This candidate explains why the sample is restricted and why the sample cannot be generalised. There is elaboration and understanding, and the answer is worth maximum marks.

Bandura et al.

(a) From the study by Bandura, Ross and Ross on aggression, briefly describe the procedure in the aggressive condition. (2 marks)

e This question asks for a description, so some detail is required. However, it is a difficult question because the procedure is long and very detailed, and it is impossible to include all of it here. *Think!* What are the most important aspects of the procedure that you should include in your answer? The use of the word 'describe' means that this is an AO1 question.

(b) From the study by Bandura, Ross and Ross on aggression, suggest why it is important to standardise a procedure. (2 marks)

e This question is tapping into your general knowledge of the methodological aspects of psychology. In this case, the question refers to the Bandura et al. study, but it could be applied to any of the core studies.

Candidates will probably include references to the control of variables, to make the dependent variable more likely to be caused by the independent variable and not to some confounding variable. As a *suggestion* is required, this is an evaluative AO2 question.

■ ■ ■

Answer to question 2: candidate A

(a) The procedure of the aggressive condition was where the child was placed in a room with an aggressive model for a period of 20 minutes. The model acted out a series of standardised physical and verbally aggressive acts, while the child observed. These acts included hitting the Bobo doll with a mallet.

e The candidate has selected appropriate aspects from the procedure to write about. The child was placed in a room for 20 minutes; the acts were standardised, and they were both physical and verbal. The child did observe these acts, which involved using a mallet. While there is much more that the candidate could have written about, there is more than enough here for maximum marks.

(b) It is important to standardise a procedure so that accurate results according to different sexes, i.e. boys and girls, can be obtained. This was done to check whether aggressiveness is learned through imitation or not.

e The candidate has written an ambiguous answer. It is correct that a procedure is standardised to obtain accurate results, but nothing more is said about it. In addition, it is unclear why the candidate refers to boys and girls, except that they were mentioned in the context of the Bandura et al. study. The candidate notes that the procedure was to check whether aggressiveness is learned through imitation,

but this just repeats the 'accurate results' comment. 1 mark is awarded for this answer.

■ ■ ■

Answer to question 2: candidate B

(a) In the aggressive condition, the child was taken into the second room and allowed to play for 5 minutes. The experimenter would tell the child that these were good toys and they were being saved for the other children. They were then taken into the third room where they were observed by observers for aggressive actions which they had copied from the aggressive model earlier.

The candidate has selected appropriate aspects of the procedure to write about, even though they are very different from those of candidate A. The children were indeed exposed to mild arousal in a second room, and they were then taken to a third room for observation. All aspects of this answer are correct, and it is worth 2 marks. Note that any mark scheme is sufficiently flexible to allow different answers, and that examiners will be briefed on this. Furthermore, examiners will know the study in all its detail, and will realise that both answers are correct and worth maximum marks.

(b) Procedures need to be standardised to ensure that all of the participants go through the same procedure. This prevents other confounding variables, such as experimenter bias or demand characteristics, from influencing behaviour. The results will not be valid or reliable if a procedure is not standardised.

This is an excellent answer, and receives 2 marks. The candidate clearly understands about standardising procedures and he or she has included appropriate terms and concepts in the answer.

Dement and Kleitman

(a) One study by Dement and Kleitman looked at the relationship between eye movements and dream content. Briefly describe the dream content for one participant. (2 marks)

> There were five different dreams reported by participants for different types of eye movement, and Dement and Kleitman report these as follows: Participant 1: standing at the bottom of a cliff operating a hoist and looking at climbers; P2: climbing ladders and looking up and down; P3 throwing basketballs at a net; P4: two people throwing tomatoes at each other; P5: driving a car then seeing a speeding car appearing from the left. The use of the word 'describe' means this is an AO1 question.

(b) One study by Dement and Kleitman looked at the relationship between eye movements and dream content. What did Dement and Kleitman conclude about the relationship between eye movements and dream content? (2 marks)

> Candidates could reply with a general comment that dream content does correspond to eye movements during sleep. Alternatively, they could reach a more specific conclusion that mainly vertical eye movement corresponds to a 'vertical' dream, and mainly horizontal movement corresponds to a 'horizontal' dream etc. This is an AO1 question because it involves recall of knowledge.

■ ■ ■

Answer to question 3: candidate A

(a) One of the participants was woken up in an interval of 5 or 15 minutes as soon as he had eye movements, and was asked if he was dreaming or recalled any dream.

> The candidate has misread the question and focused on the second of Dement and Kleitman's aims rather than the third. Although what is written is correct, it does not answer the question and scores 0 marks.

(b) Dement and Kleitman concluded that eye movements (vertical, horizontal etc., none, or a combination of both) were significantly related to the content of the dream.

> This a good answer: clear concise, accurate, and worth 2 marks.

Answer to question 3: candidate B

(a) When eye movement was vertical, participants reported climbing ladders and looking down, or aiming a ball at a basketball net.

> The answer receives maximum marks, because the candidate identifies vertical eye movement and two corresponding dreams with some accuracy.

question

(b) They concluded that dream content correlates with the type of REM movement. For example, vertical REM — looking at a basketball hoop, and little or no REM — looking at objects in the distance.

e This answer receives maximum marks because the candidate provides a conclusion and supports the answer with two relevant examples.

Baron-Cohen et al.

(a) The 1997 core study by Baron-Cohen et al. on autism was updated 4 years later. Briefly discuss two problems with the original (1997) eyes test. (4 marks)

In their 2001 paper, Baron-Cohen et al. list eight problems with the original (1997) version of the eyes test. The OCR specification states that 'candidates will be asked questions relating to research surrounding the core studies', and so to ask a question about later research on the same thing is perfectly acceptable. It is not possible to reproduce here all the eight problems and so a reference to the article itself is advised. This is an AO2 question because it requires *discussion*.

■ ■ ■

Answer to question 5: candidate A

(a) The 1997 version had a forced choice of two answers, which is too narrow. For example, one set of eyes had serious or playful, and the answer was obvious. The updated version had four choices of serious, ashamed, alarmed and bewildered, which was more difficult and less narrow. Second, the original test had more female faces than male faces, and this may have biased the result. In the later version there were equal numbers of male and female faces, so this variable was controlled and gender of face could not confound the result.

This is an excellent answer. The first example is correct, and although there could have been a little more discussion, the candidate has clearly compared the two versions accurately. The second point is also excellent because not only is the update clearly outlined, but there is also knowledge of the implications and familiarity with the appropriate terminology. Overall, this answer gains maximum marks.

Answer to question 5: candidate B

(a) Two problems were first that the 1997 version had a forced choice of answers and second that there were more female faces than male faces.

Two problems are *identified* here and both are correct. However, the question requires that the problems be *discussed* and candidate B does not do that. However, this is a partially correct answer and so 2 marks are awarded out of the 4 marks available. You must answer the question set and include sufficient detail to score maximum marks. A comparison of this answer with that of candidate A will make clear why candidate A was awarded more marks than candidate B.

Griffiths

(a) The study by Griffiths on fruit-machine gambling used the 'thinking aloud' method. Describe two categories of verbalisation/utterance. (2 marks)

This is an AO1 question, and it is a 'two things for 2 marks' question. It should be easy because all you have to do is to recall two of the 30 categories. (Read the article for yourself if you want to know what they are).

■ ■ ■

Answer to question 4: candidate A

(a) Two categories were when the person said no, and when the person said yes.

You may not believe this, but this answer must be awarded 2 marks. Category 9 was 'saying no', and category 10 was 'saying yes'. So this is a brief but correct answer.

■ ■ ■

Answer to question 4: candidate B

(a) The first category was 'Personification of the fruit machines', such as when the person would say 'the machine likes me', and the second category was 'Explaining away losses', for example, the gambler may state 'I lost there because I wasn't concentrating'.

This candidate has taken the first two verbalisation categories straight from the article and reproduced them word for word. The candidate has also quoted the examples directly from the article. This is an impressive answer, but it can still only score the 2 marks available.

Rosenhan

(a) The study by Rosenhan (sane in insane places) suggests that doctors are strongly biased toward type two errors. What is a type two error? (2 marks)

> A type two error is calling a healthy person sick (a false negative). In the Rosenhan study, this involves labelling the pseudo-patient as schizophrenic when he/she is not.

(b) The study by Rosenhan (sane in insane places) suggests that doctors are strongly biased toward type two errors. Suggest why doctors have this bias. (2 marks)

> Doctors should avoid type one errors at all costs. This would be to say an ill person is healthy, and so is negligent. To be accurate is best (i.e. to say that an ill person is ill and a healthy person is healthy). But if there is doubt, as in this study, the best strategy is to make a type two error — to be safe rather than sorry.

■ ■ ■

Answer to question 6: candidate A

(a) The psychiatrists labelled the patients as schizophrenic, because psychiatrists cannot tell the difference between sane and insane people.

> The candidate does not answer the question directly, as he or she does not define a type two error. However, the first part of the answer is correct because the candidate has provided an example of a type two error, i.e. the psychiatrists mislabelling the patients as schizophrenic when they were not. This answer scores 1 mark.

(b) The psychiatrists are biased because they are the ones with the knowledge, and they assume that they are right. They are not competent because they judge the sane person to be insane and this is a type two error.

> The first part of the answer is not the way to evaluate (see the 'Evaluation' section on p. 41). The comment about competence is also inappropriate. However, although the reasoning behind the answer is incorrect, the candidate correctly identifies what a type two error is and so scores 1 mark.

■ ■ ■

Answer to question 6: candidate B

(a) A type two error is the safe option. It is when a healthy person is labelled as sick when the healthy person is really healthy, such as labelling the pseudo-patients as schizophrenic when they are not. A type one error is the opposite, when a sick person is labelled as healthy.

> This is a really good answer because the candidate knows what a type two error is and he or she has elaborated by providing an example. Although it is not

question

required, the candidate shows his or her understanding by providing a definition of a type one error.

(b) Psychiatrists have a responsibility to both the community and the patient. If there is any doubt about whether a person is ill, then they should assume there is a problem, in this case assume the patient is schizophrenic and admit him/her. The pseudo-patients did report that they were hearing voices and this is not normal, so what else were they to assume? Admitting them for further tests or observation shows competence and responsibility and the safer type two error. The worst thing would be to send an ill person back on to the streets, which would be a type one error.

🖉 The candidate really understands both type one and type two errors and how they relate to the Rosenhan study. This is an excellent answer and it scores full marks.

7

Piliavin et al.

Choose one of the following core studies and answer the questions below:

- **Piliavin et al. (subway Samaritans)**
- **Baron-Cohen et al. (eyes test)**

(a) What was the aim of your chosen study? (2 marks)
(b) Briefly outline the background to your chosen study. (6 marks)
(c) Describe how quantitative data were gathered in your chosen study. (6 marks)
(d) Give one advantage and one disadvantage of quantitative data. (6 marks)
(e) Outline the results of your chosen study. (8 marks)
(f) Suggest two changes to your chosen study, and outline any methodological implications that these changes may have. (8 marks)

■ ■ ■

Answer to question 7: candidate A

(a) The aim of the 'Subway Samaritans' study conducted by Piliavin et al. was to investigate the differences in helping behaviour (helping someone up) on a New York subway train, according to whether the person requiring help appeared drunk or ill, and was either black or white.

> *e* This answer scores full marks. The candidate knows that the study is on helping behaviour, and understands the appropriate variables of drunk/ill and black/white.

(b) The research was prompted by the brutal murder of Kitty Genovese outside her own home in Queens during 1964. The woman was not killed immediately and had time to call out for help several times, but, despite this fact, none of the 38 people who observed the stabbing from their windows intervened or helped directly. The incident was later explained by the principle of 'diffusion of responsibility', whereby the more people that are present when witnessing such an event, the less likely each of them are to help, since they feel less accountable personally, and the responsibility is divided among the larger group of people. Piliavin, therefore, wanted to conduct further research into helping behaviour, namely whether city dwellers are inherently good and will help someone who falls over, or whether diffusion of responsibility inevitably occurs in most urban situations.

> *e* This answer would certainly score 5–6 marks. There could have been a comment about the laboratory experiments that followed the murder, but what is written is of very good quality.

(c) Quantitative data were gathered as experimenters entered a New York subway train in groups of four. One experimenter would play a stooge, appearing ill, by means of a cane, or drunk by dressing scruffily; the second was a helper who would aid the stooge after an allotted time had passed without help; and the two remaining experimenters were observers who seated themselves in the same carriage as the planned fall, or in the adjacent one. Out of the experimenters used, at least one had a different ethnicity, in order to observe how this variable affected helping behaviour, when playing the stooge. The stooge would enter the subway carriage, and appear to fall over in the central area. Then experimenters would observe the time taken for help to be offered, the frequency that help was offered, and the sex and ethnicity of the helper.

> The candidate does not explicitly define qualitative data, but, from what is written, it is clear that he or she knows what it is. When describing how the data were gathered in the study, the candidate mentions the train, the victim's conditions, the observers, and some of the response categories in which the data were recorded. While the answer is clear, it does not answer the question fully. More could be said about the observers and the response categories. However, it scores 5 out of 6 marks.

(d) One advantage of quantitative data is that they are objective, and could therefore be seen as a much more scientific measure than qualitative data. Measures of central tendency and dispersion can be applied, allowing for greater analysis of data, whereby the trends can be observed and the conclusions can be backed up by empirical evidence.

One disadvantage of quantitative data, however, is that they can be deemed reductionist, since they simplify otherwise complex behaviour into mere facts and figures. Through a purely quantitative approach, it is unlikely that the reasons for target behaviours can be discovered, merely the trends that the behaviour takes.

> The candidate gives an advantage of quantitative data, and comments that they are more objective and scientific. This advantage is described rather than identified. The candidate then provides elaboration, and shows good understanding of psychological terminology when adding details of measures of central tendency etc. The disadvantage follows the same pattern. The disadvantage is appropriate, clear, and there is elaboration and understanding. This answer gains maximum marks.

(e) Experimenters found great differences between the ill and drunk conditions of the experiment: for example, the ill condition received spontaneous help 95% of the time, whereas the drunken stooge was only helped 50%. The time that it took before help was offered also varied greatly, with the average time for the ill condition being 5 seconds, but, for the drunk condition, participants waited for as long as 109 seconds before offering help. It was also found that participants were much more likely to help a person of their own ethnicity or sex. Diffusion of responsibility did not occur, however, since the participants were face to face with the stooge, and therefore felt directly accountable, however many people there were surrounding them.

> The question requires details about only the results of the study, so any other information, such as procedure, would not be relevant. The candidate answers the question specifically and provides actual figures for a number of dependent variables. The candidate also comments on the 'diffusion of responsibility'

hypothesis. This is an impressive answer, showing accuracy and understanding. This answer scores 8 marks.

(f) Participants could have been given self-report questionnaires upon leaving the subway train. This would have allowed participants to express their own feelings about the study, thus providing qualitative data, and it would also make the study more ethical, since it would act as a kind of debrief, whereas originally participants had no idea that they were taking part in a psychological study. This measure however, would probably have resulted in a higher percentage of helping for both conditions, since questionnaires are subjective and participants are much more likely to provide socially desirable answers, claiming that they would carry out behaviour, rather than actually exhibiting it during the event. The finding that 95% helped the ill stooge would probably be increased to 100%, because who would say that they would not help an ill man?

🖉 This is a superb answer that scores maximum marks. It has everything that is needed, plus some more.

Additionally, the experiment could have been carried out as a double-blind study, whereby the observers would not know the aim of the study and would therefore be more impartial. Previously, since the observers were looking for a large disparity between results of the ill and drunk conditions, they may have felt a tendency to underestimate or overestimate times in order to fit their hypotheses better. This change therefore, would have increased the validity of the results, since an impartial observer would be merely noting down the behaviour he has been told to, and results are not clouded by extraneous variables such as observer bias. This would probably have resulted in slightly lower frequency of helping for the ill condition and slightly higher for the drunk condition.

🖉 This is an interesting variation, and the answer shows the understanding that the candidate has. Particularly impressive is the use of psychological terminology and concepts; for example, the candidate clearly knows what validity is.

■ ■ ■

Answer to question 7: candidate B

(a) The aim of the study was to look at how being on a subway train turned people into a subway Samaritan.

🖉 This answer scores just 1 mark. The candidate has some idea about the content of the study, but does not elaborate on the basic idea.

(b) Kitty Genovese got killed, and although people heard her screaming, they couldn't be bothered to help or even call the police. This was called bystander apathy, even though the people weren't bystanding, but in their houses. This led to lots of research being done to investigate it, but being psychologists they did it in a lab. The lab studies found that people didn't help the victim. Ethics is a relevant issue in psychology, and the lab experiments involved participants being deceived. They thought that a victim was in need, whereas the victim wasn't really in need; it was all just an act.

> The candidate knows the gist of the background to the study, but the answer is rather vague. The murder is mentioned, and there is a comment about bystanders. The candidate knows that laboratory studies were then done, but does not say much about the experiments, except that they were unethical. The laboratory studies did involve deception, but this is only peripherally relevant. This answer achieves 3–4 marks.

(c) Quantitative data were gathered by the observers on the train. One sat in the adjacent carriage and the other sat in the critical area carriage. Both observers recorded what happened, and then later they compared their results for inter-rater reliability.

> Quantitative data were gathered by the observers, but they did not sit as suggested — both sat in the adjacent carriage. The observers did not record the same thing; instead, they recorded different things. This means that they could not compare data for inter-rater reliability. So, although the answer *sounds* good, it is not, and it achieves no more than 1–2 marks.

(d) An advantage of quantitative data is that it uses numbers. If numbers are used, then percentages can be calculated and statistical tests applied, and this makes the data more scientific.

A disadvantage is that Piliavin didn't ask the people on the train why they helped or didn't help. This would have given more insight, and doing this would have been good.

> The candidate gives an advantage of quantitative data, in that statistics etc. can be applied. This is correct, but there is very little/no elaboration, so this part of the answer achieves 2 marks. The disadvantage is a correct example of how *qualitative* data could have been gathered, but this is not a disadvantage of *quantitative* data. No marks are awarded for the disadvantage.

(e) The results were not as expected. They thought that no one would help because they had the models on stand-by. However, most people did help. More people helped the ill victim than the drunk victim — nearly 90%.

> This is a very brief answer, but what is written is correct. It is basic and lacks detail, but there is some understanding. It scores 3 marks.

(f) One change is that they could have done the study on a different train. I know they chose the train because it was a fixed time, but I'm sure they could find a different subway in the whole of New York. This means that the participants would not be the same every day. In fact they would have to use different trains because if they chose one other line, the same participants may get on that train every day. Oops! If there were different participants then the results may have been different.

This is an interesting answer, as the candidate makes a suggestion and then realises it has not been fully thought through before beginning to write about it. Using the same train could be a problem, and alternative trains could run through different parts of the city, carrying different types of people. This is a reasonable suggestion, and scores maximum marks for this part of the question. The comment about results is too vague, and scores no marks at all.

Another change would be to do a different method altogether. You could go to a station to make it authentic, and then ask people: 'if someone fell over on a train, and they were ill (or drunk), would you get up and help them?' They could answer yes or no. This would give qualitative data rather than quantitative data. The implication is that the reliability and validity would be improved.

This is a good alternative, and the candidate scores both of the available marks for describing this change. For the implications part of the question, the candidate merely states that this would improve reliability and validity, without saying how and without showing that he or she understands what the terms mean. It is doubtful whether reliability and validity would actually improve. There are no marks for the implications component.

Samuel and Bryant

(a) **Outline one assumption of the developmental approach in psychology.** (2 marks)

(b) **Describe how the developmental approach could explain the ability to conserve.** (4 marks)

(c) **Describe one similarity and one difference between the Samuel and Bryant study and any other developmental study.** (6 marks)

(d) **Discuss the strengths and limitations of the developmental approach, using examples from the Samuel and Bryant study.** (12 marks)

Answer to question 8: candidate A

(a) One assumption of the developmental approach is that psychologists can generalise findings from children to adults.

> This is a brief answer that is rather ambiguous. One school of thought suggests that children are merely adults in miniature, but another suggests that children are very different from adults and cannot be generalised. As the assumption is ambiguous and brief, it scores 1 mark.

(b) The Samuel and Bryant study investigated the ability of children to conserve by forming several conditions, grouping the children by age. They were shown a conservation task, and it was then recorded whether the child made an error or not when asked which container has more fluid in it. It was found that the youngest children made the most errors, and the number of errors then decreased when older children were used. This suggests that ability to conserve comes with age, the mean of which in this case was around 7 years old.

> This is a very good answer and worth all the available marks. There is good knowledge of the Samuel and Bryant study, and the candidate understands what he or she is writing about. There is accurate knowledge of the recording of errors and the conservation tasks too. The candidate has answered the question precisely, by providing an explanation that younger children made most errors, but that the errors decreased as the children got older, thus concluding that the ability to conserve improves as the child develops.

(c) A similarity between the Samuel and Bryant study and Bandura's study on aggression in children is that they were both conducted in a laboratory. This allowed for control over extraneous variables, but also gave both studies relatively low ecological validity. A difference between these two studies, however, is that Bandura's study was highly unethical, since children had to witness violence and were then encouraged to reproduce it themselves. The Samuel and Bryant study, on the other hand, was entirely ethical, with children performing a task which was simple and did not cause them any harm.

> This is a superb answer. Both studies were conducted in a laboratory (1 mark scored for a basic answer), and this did give control over the extraneous variables. Moreover, the candidate includes a comment about low ecological validity, which is correct for both studies. The candidate clearly elaborates on the similarities between the two studies. The differences are also pertinent. The Bandura study was indeed unethical (and the reasons why are stated), and the Samuel and Bryant study was ethical (and the reasons again are stated).

(d) There are a number of strengths to the developmental approach as shown by the Samuel and Bryant study, such as the fact that it uses a wide range of children from different ages, so that it can be found at what age a behaviour starts to be exhibited. For example, in this study, it was found that the mean age that children start to conserve is 7 years old, and this finding could not have been found without studying children of a variety of ages. The approach therefore provides guidelines for which parents can expect to see their children exhibiting certain behaviours.

> The question requires strengths (plural), so at least two should be included. There is an example from the Samuel and Bryant study, but the strength is not isolated. The final comment could be a strength: 'providing guidelines for parents', but there is no supporting example or discussion of it. This is generally a poor answer so far.

There are numerous weaknesses to the approach, however, for example, working with children can reduce the validity of results, since they may misinterpret experimenters' questions. Experimenters therefore have to ensure that the task carried out by the children for them is simple enough to understand. The Samuel and Bryant study ensured this by using materials which children would be familiar with, such as plasticine and counters. Another weakness is that results cannot always be generalised, as children should not be considered the same as adults. In addition, any research conducted on children of a certain generation may not have been true for the previous generation when they were children, so studies need to be repeated frequently. In the Samuel and Bryant study it was generalised that children can conserve from the age of 7 and above, but we do not know if this was true for children of a previous generation. Societies differ greatly over time, and if nurture is to be regarded as an important factor in development, then behaviour could have changed greatly over this time period.

> This part of the answer is much better. There are a number of weaknesses provided (misinterpretation of questions, cannot generalise to adults, and cannot generalise from one generation to another), and each of these has supporting examples with some discussion.

> Overall, there is an imbalance of strengths and weaknesses. However, there are some supporting examples and some discussion, and the understanding is good. This answer would just creep into the 7–9 mark band.

■ ■ ■

Answer to question 8: candidate B

(a) One assumption of the developmental approach is that if development is studied in the same individual over a period of time, as in a longitudinal study, then any changes in behaviour can be recorded and studied. Another assumption is that development takes place throughout a person's life and it is not just a childhood thing.

> The question only requires one assumption and, perhaps just for luck, two are thrown in by the candidate. Candidates sometimes do this to cover themselves. In this case, either assumption could score marks. The first has more detail and scores full marks. The second is also correct, but it lacks detail.

(b) The ability to conserve was shown in the Samuel and Bryant study. They looked at a number of methodological problems raised in the work of Piaget. They looked at the conservation of volume (liquid), of mass (plasticine) and number (using counters). They looked at whether children should be asked one question, as Piaget did, or whether children should only be asked two questions. They also looked at different ages.

> The candidate knows what went on in this study and provides a lot of accurate detail. He or she refers to the three main variables that Samuel and Bryant looked at — all correctly described. However, the candidate does not answer the question. There is no reference to any developmental process here. Section C questions are not about the details of specific studies, but are about using the studies as examples of approaches, issues, methods and perspectives. *Think!* The crucial point is to relate the study to *development*. Candidate A does this, while candidate B does not. Some marks are scored by candidate B, but not top-band marks.

(c) A similarity between the Samuel and Bryant study and Bandura's study is that they are both on children, and participants under 16 years of age cannot give informed consent. Samuel and Bryant used children aged between 5 and 8 years old, and the children chosen by Bandura were even younger. Although neither study specifies it, consent would have been obtained from the parents of the children, or from their schoolteachers acting *in loco parentis*.

A difference between the two studies is that Samuel and Bryant (and Piaget before them) showed that cognitive processes develop and can't be taught. The age may be in question, but it is not something that can be taught to all 4-year-olds for example. Bandura was different, because he showed that aggression can be taught. It isn't something that develops, but can be taught at any age. It's like a toddler who bumps into a chair, cries, and the parent tells the child to smack the naughty chair.

> This is a superb answer. The similarity is an appropriate one, and there is elaboration that is entirely correct. The difference is appropriate too, and the candidate elaborates on this too.

(d) There are a number of strengths to the developmental approach as shown by the Samuel and Bryant study. For example, changes in cognitive or any other form of development can be recorded over time. In the Samuel and Bryant study, although they didn't study the same children over time, they took the next-best option and studied children of different ages to see if the older children had developed.

Another strength is that it can show us how best to educate children. The Samuel and Bryant study showed us what younger children cannot do, so there is no point in trying to teach certain things to younger children. Another strength is that if a longitudinal study is done, we can really see changes in an individual. Samuel and Bryant didn't do this, but, if they had done, it would have been much better. If they had tested the same child every day, they would know if the child developed the ability to conserve overnight or not.

ℯ This is a good answer, with a number of appropriate strengths and an example to support each. There are the beginnings of a discussion about testing the same child each day but, other than this, discussion is rather sparse.

There are a number of weaknesses to the developmental approach. There is the problem of communication. Children cannot communicate their thoughts and feelings clearly. They may become confused, and may misinterpret what is required, e.g. asking only one question. Another weakness is a problem of inter-pretation. Experimenters may misinterpret what a child intends, e.g. Hans's father and/or Freud may misinterpret. Finally, studies on development take time — one way to study development over time is to do a longitudinal study, but this takes time; or snapshot studies are done, comparing one child with another, which is what Samuel and Bryant did.

ℯ The candidate focuses his or her answer on the methodological problems, but this is not a problem. However, the examples given do not always refer to the Samuel and Bryant study as the question requires. There is not much discussion either.

Overall, there is a balance of strengths and weaknesses, and each point is supported with an example. The candidate understands the Samuel and Bryant study. Discussion could be better, and so the answer would be at the top end of the 7–9 mark band.